The Urban Handbook

BTCV is the UK's leading practical conservation charity. We support the activities of more than 140,000 volunteers every year, who take part in projects and come from all sections of the community to do practical conservation in the UK and worldwide. BTCV runs a programme of training courses, many of which are designed to help people put the theory contained in the Practical Handbook series into practice. For information about any of BTCV's volunteering opportunities, please contact BTCV at the address below.

Other titles in BTCV's
Practical Handbook series:

Dry Stone Walling

Fencing

Footpaths

Hedging

Sand Dunes

Tool Care

Tree Planting and Aftercare

Waterways and Wetlands

Woodlands

To order any of these, or for details of other BTCV publications and merchandise, please contact:

BTCV Enterprises Ltd.,
Sedum House, Mallard Way,
Doncaster DN4 8DB
Tel: 01302 388883

www.btcv.org/shop

The Urban Handbook
a practical guide to community
environmental work

Elizabeth Agate

BTCV

BTCV would like to thank the following individuals who have contributed their advice and experience:

George Barker, Karl Bartlett, Rob Bowker, Andrew Brown, Richard Butcher, Dave Carr, Patrick Crowley, Phil Dickin, Dave Dutton, Paul Forrest-Jameson, Nick Forster, Jenni French, Meg Game, James Graham, Dean Heward, Polly Hearsey, Mark Joslyn, Hazel Kirby, Noel Lowry, Tean Mitchell, Jo Mercer, Jim O'Shaughnessy, John Preston, Adele Ratcliffe, Melanie Rowe, Charles Rugeroni, Andy Stokes, Mark Spriggs, Marion Vere.

BTCV acknowledges financial support from Barclays PLC
in the development of this handbook

ISBN   0   946752   15   X

Written by Elizabeth Agate
with Introduction and Chapter 1 by Tean Mitchell

Illustrations by Linda Francis

Cover: Phoenix Community Garden, London.
Photos: Phil Harrison and Jane Alexander

First published May 1998
Appendices revised April 2002, May 2007

© BTCV 1998-2007

1   3   5   7   9   8   6   4   2

BTCV acknowledges support from the Cabinet Office, Office of the Third Sector

Printed by Wrightsons Ltd., Northamptonshire on recycled paper.

Published by BTCV, Sedum House, Mallard Way, Doncaster DN4 8DB
Telephone: 01302 388883
Registered Charity 261009

Foreword

Of all the people on the Earth today, one in one hundred is living in the British Isles. This is a very crowded part of the world, and the vast majority of us live an extremely urban lifestyle. For many young children and older people, their familiar physical environment rarely stretches further than the end of the street – or if they're lucky, to their garden, the local park, or a nearby patch of 'unofficial' urban wildspace.

Whilst our physical horizons may be very local, the full environmental impact of urban lifestyle extends way beyond the city boundary. Much of the produce which we consume will have travelled halfway around the world before we buy it, and the effect of the waste we generate has an impact on the farthest corners of the oceans. Our chemical pollution even weakens the Earth's protective ozone layer.

No one disputes the need to motivate the people of the world to make amends and minimise their global impact, but the process needs to start on home ground, where the problems are easy to see, and where action delivers encouragingly tangible results. In an urban community such as ours, it must make sense to focus action on the physical surroundings in the towns and cities where we live and work. This is the place where conservation skills should be taught, where more inventive management of resources can best be fostered, and where most of us can play an active part in helping the Earth to get better.

In global terms, the lessons we can learn in urban Britain have a particularly powerful role to play. Even in the most rural of developing countries, the trend is inevitably towards a life in towns for more and more people. Urban environmental action is one really valuable contribution we can make to international conservation, and to achieving greater long-term sustainability on a world-wide scale.

It would be a mistake to think that environmental action in towns is little more than a pale version of the genuine article. The direct rewards of urban environmental action are very real. Urban journeys are short, and most have no need for a motor vehicle. Urban allotments and vegetable gardens have far greater productivity potential than even the most intensive of rural farming. Buildings and land in towns are frequently recycled. This is where we have the greatest scope for capturing energy from the sun and for utilising storm-water run-off. Even the more traditional conservationist's interest in wildlife is well served in towns. There is a spectactular diversity of species in our gardens, and great scope for creating new habitats through urban forestry, park meadow management, and multi-functional wetlands which can clean waste water and accommodate both junior pond-dippers and endangered dragonflies.

The conservation focus has been far too rural for far too long. Of course we need to care for the countryside and conserve rare wildlife in the remote corners of the British Isles, but we must make much more effort to improve the quality of life in urban Britain. We must engage many more people in the practical business of working in partnership, to make a difference on the doorstep. Despite its rural reputation, BTCV has a long and honourable history of local environmental action in urban areas. This handbook celebrates that track-record, offers a wealth of practical experience, and will help enormously in capturing the hearts and minds of those millions of us who live and work in towns, and encouraging us to practical action.

Chris Baines
Wolverhampton, 1997

Contents

List of plates

Plate 1: Abbot's Wood, Bristol;
Laurel Glen, South Belfast

Plate 2: Bury, Lancashire; Bristol, Avon;
Tree dressing, Brixton

Plate 3: Prestwich Forest Park, Lancashire

Plate 4: Low Brankin Moor Ecology Park,
Darlington; Forest Fields Play Centre Nature
Garden, Nottingham

Plate 5: Craigton Cemetery, Glasgow;
Beersbridge Nature Walk, Belfast; Captain's
Clough, Bolton

Plate 6: Gomm's Wood, High Wycombe;

Plate 7: Huddersfield, West Yorkshire

Plate 8: Bolton Wildlife Project

Plate 9: Flora; Belfast Wildflower Nursery

Plate 10: Hollybush Farm Wildlife Garden, Leeds

Plate 11: Springfield Community Garden,
Bradford

Plate 12: Brixton LETS EAT Group; Newham
Community Project, St. Anthony's School

Plate 13: [Eldon & Seaside]

Introduction

Recognising the unique qualities of cities and towns is an important first step in understanding how best to contribute to environmental improvements. Diversity is what makes cities special. West Indian grocers jostle Chinese supermarkets, Portuguese cafés and the Asian Community Action office sit alongside the English butchers and the Irish pub. The very diversity of the human population in cities, its multi-cultural nature, has led to lateral thinking by conservationists. While the need and desire to green the city and provide wildlife habitats is a major force behind urban conservation work, bringing relevance to your activities to involve a wide range of people in environmental action means taking an imaginative approach. In many city projects, consciousness-raising is just as important as practical conservation. Helping school children create a nature mural or design a cultural flower bed of plants from the West Indies may be just as valuable as tree planting with a residents' group or creating a nature area with a group of conservation volunteers.

The breadth of work and the range of communities with which BTCV is now involved has expanded greatly in the past few years. They range from people on a housing estate trying to brighten the place up; a community group growing its own food; the patients and staff of a doctor's surgery creating a physic garden; the local Chinese Community group encouraging their old folk to take up gardening; the church congregation turning their churchyard into a wildlife haven; or a 'Friends of.....' group taking on the practical management of a remnant ancient woodland. From window boxes to woodlands, via nature murals and tree dressing, the activities of the urban conservationist are as diverse as the population itself. Recycling, composting and community art have joined the long list of activities of the urban conservationist.

Conserving and enhancing biodiversity is still high on the agenda. Cities, towns and suburbs are incredibly rich in wildlife, with a greater range of habitats than intensively farmed 'countryside'. You're more likely to see a fox in the town than in the country, and kestrels are common hovering above roadside verges. A pair of sparrowhawks has nested in the plane trees of a South London street, and hundreds of newts were discovered in a city school pond. On a hedge in a city school nature area five different wasp galls were found on just one plant, proving that biodiversity is alive and well and living in the city. Where the urban conservationist has been at work, you could visit a rich summer meadow, an ancient coppice woodland, a newly-laid hedge or a wetland teeming with life – all in just one afternoon.

School nature areas, community wildlife gardens and other similar areas are often small. Maintaining many different habitats in such small spaces, often under great human pressure, creates a need for particularly intensive management. While such a level of management is usually seen in negative terms, in cities this is a positive asset, providing lots of opportunities for active participation, training, practical conservation, education and community involvement.

The key to successful city greening is community action. Urban conservation is all about local people doing something in their own locality with their neighbours, friends, work mates or club members, often with a knock-on benefit to the rest of the community. The taking part can be as important as the end product. The creation of a community garden for a block of single person flats can lead to communication and exchange among the residents who might seldom have made contact in the past.

This handbook is aimed at anyone who is interested in urban environmental action, from the concerned individual, through to project officers with responsibility for encouraging community action. The handbook begins by looking at how communities function, and gives lots of ideas for getting started with days of action and other short term projects. Chapter 3 looks in detail at how people interact with green spaces in urban areas, how they perceive them, use them, and at the effect management has on them. It also discusses the issues of local ownership and vandalism. Chapter 4 describes the range of habitats found in towns and cities, many of which are special to urban areas, and how they are affected by soils, climate and other factors. Chapters 5-10 give advice on a wide range of practical environmental work, from rubbish clearance, to fencing, tree planting, pond creation, nestbox construction and many others. Information on health, safety and tools is given in an appendix.

Examples of projects by BTCV and other groups are included throughout the book. References to other publications in the text are given by author and date, or title, publisher and date, according to their listing in the bibliography.

4   Features of urban habitats

Urban habitats have many features which differentiate them from rural semi-natural habitats. Management and creation of urban habitats is not necessarily about recreating pieces of countryside, but about making the most of the unique features which urban habitats present.

Site surveys

This chapter describes the valuable range of features which urban green spaces contain. Before any decisions are made about practical work on sites, it's important to find out what is there already. Site surveys should include the flora and fauna, soil and exposures of rock. The industrial or land use history of the site is also important, not only for its part in local history, but for understanding the way in which plant and animal communities have developed on the site.

In the last decade, the interest in urban wildlife has grown enormously, and many towns and cities have active urban wildlife groups who have surveyed the green spaces in their local area, and compiled species lists for some sites. Some county wildlife trusts and the statutory nature conservation bodies have staff with particular responsibilities for urban areas. Local authorities or museums may be responsible for biological databases. There is already a fund of knowledge about many areas, and the first move when considering surveying a site should always be to check for existing information, through the above organisations. Most areas have standard methods for surveying and recording, which should be followed, so further monitoring and comparisons with other sites can be usefully carried out.

Site surveys can be done at two levels. The first level is a general survey of the site, recording a general site description, natural history observations and the site history. The site is then divided into parcels of distinct habitat or management type, and each parcel is checked for a range of characteristics, including bare ground, vegetation types, water, substrate, drainage and land use. A sketch map is made to show the boundaries, adjacent land use, access and other features. This initial survey indicates the areas of natural history interest which need further surveying.

The second level of survey is to record species of flora and fauna present, concentrating on those groups for which the site appears to be valuable. Quantitative data, which indicates the amount or frequency of each particular species, is helpful. Flora, birds and butterflies are the easiest to record, and it should not be difficult to find someone able to do this. More specialist knowledge and skills are required for recording mammals, reptiles, amphibians, fish, invertebrates, fungi, ferns, mosses and lichens.

This knowledge provides a basis for informed discussion about the site, and gives a base line for future monitoring. Such a survey should be objective and accurate, but the value which different people place on the various species, and how any management may affect them, may be subject to further discussion between different interest groups. The site also needs to be assessed in relation to other sites in the area. If it is uncommon in the area, this may increase its value. On the other hand, sites that are small and isolated from other similar sites may not be able to support viable populations. See the section on size and isolation, on page 34.

Soils and substrates

Parks, commons, and areas of ancient habitat such as semi-natural woodlands may have soils that are entirely natural and have received very little human disturbance. Other areas, particularly abandoned industrial sites, sites of demolished buildings, and road and railway embankments have soils and substrates which have been greatly altered. Many sites have no topsoil, but comprise building rubble, concrete, Tarmac, and tips of industrial waste and mining waste, some of which cover huge areas. Site factors may include absence or shallow depth of workable topsoil, poor aeration, stoniness, extremes of pH, electrical conductivity, heavy metal content, iron pyrite content or organic contaminants. These characteristics are not necessarily problems, and many such sites support an interesting and even spectacular assemblage of plants (p32). Generally, sites with 'poor' soils and low fertility produce, in the initial stages of succession, a more varied and interesting flora and fauna than sites of higher fertility.

When considering sites in urban areas, it is important to find out the characteristics of the substrates, and generally to work with the opportunities that they present, rather than trying to impose changes which may well not be viable. In some cases, allowing any succession to continue naturally may be the best option, whilst intervening only to maintain paths or open areas, or to control undesirable invasive species.

Plants, including trees, that naturally appear on a site are nearly always more successful than introduced individuals, and on disturbed and variable soils this is even more likely to be the case. However, on some sites the need to maintain site diversity, improve appearance or site safety, or to encourage community action and use of the site, may be more important than natural succession of the habitat.

Before working on any abandoned industrial sites information should be obtained from landowners or agents about any possible hazards from polluted or hazardous substrates. The Environmental Health Department of the local authority should also be able to give advice. Methane leakage may be a problem on sites which have been used for tipping rubbish. This can cause a particular problem with pond creation, if methane bubbles form under pond liners.

Many sites have been disturbed due to the installation of underground services, which also need taking into account when planning site works (p43).

Recently farmed land, grassland or abandoned allotments tend to have deep soils and high fertility. These soils, which are good for cultivated crops, are not easy to convert to attractive semi-natural vegetation, because the fertility encourages the growth of aggressive species, which may suppress more desirable plant species that are introduced to the site. Left to themselves, these sites tend to grow over with coarse grasses, nettle, bramble, elder and other species, which although supporting a range of invertebrates, birds and mammals, may not be the best vegetation for sites intended for public access. Cropping, without the addition of fertilisers, reduces phosphate levels in the soil, but nitrogen is replenished from the air through rainfall, and in urban areas, from car exhausts, and it may be difficult to reduce soil nitrogen levels. On some sites, where the desired aim is a wildflower dominated grassland, topsoil has been removed to reduce fertility, the resulting substrate being sown with a wildflower mix (chapter 7). Success has been variable.

The creation of woodland on fertile soils is also more difficult than on poorer soils, because of the rampant weed growth which will suppress the young trees in the early years. Weeding is vital for at least five years after planting. The formation of a woodland flora is likely to be a long and slow process, and in the initial decades the developing woodland will probably be dominated by couch, false oat grass, nettle, ivy, bracken and bramble (chapter 6).

Climate

Urban areas have climates which are noticeably different from surrounding rural areas, and which in turn affect the type of flora and fauna that may flourish. The climatic differences increase with increasing size of the urban area, and show a gradient from the suburbs to the city centre.

Average temperatures are higher throughout the year, particularly at night, due to the conductive property of hard surfaces and buildings, and heat generation by industry, transport and other activities within the city. Precipitation is drained away artificially, with less absorption into the ground, giving generally drier soils. The reduced evapotranspiration means low humidity, resulting in a climate which has similarities with the Mediterranean.

This has several effects:

- The period of winter inactivity is generally shortened. Both introduced and native species of plants may flower earlier in spring, and stay in growth later into the autumn. Winter-flowering species flower well. These in turn support invertebrates, birds and animals, which may thus survive in relatively high numbers and be less liable to 'crash' in periods of severe weather. Cold winter temperatures still occur in urban areas, but in general winters are less harsh than in the rural surrounds.

- Particular species of plants and animals are able to survive further north than in rural areas, though periods of frost may cause losses. In general these species are seen as a bonus to the variety of wildlife to be found in towns.

- Periods of hot, dry weather in summer, with very low humidity and rapid drying out of soils means that habitats typical of rural areas may struggle to survive, and be difficult to create. Woodlands may fail to develop the full range of organisms which flourish in the cooler and more humid climate in rural areas. The urban flora which appears naturally on urban waste land, with its colourful burst of growth in early summer from annuals and biennials, typical pioneer shrub and tree species, and rather barren winter appearance, may indicate the type of habitat best suited to the urban climate.

Flora and fauna

The variety and extent of green spaces in urban areas results in some urban areas having a far greater proportion of semi-natural habitat than equivalent-size areas of countryside, especially those which are intensively farmed. The range of flora and fauna contained in this green space is varied and rich, with characteristics which differentiate it from the flora and fauna of rural areas.

FLORA

Many of the plant species to be found growing naturally in disturbed ground or on 'wasteland' in urban areas are ruderal or pioneer species, which are the first plants to colonise disturbed ground. Many of these species used to thrive on arable land, but some have become uncommon in the countryside due to herbicides and modern cultivation methods. On newly disturbed ground in urban areas they find a refuge, but unless the site is disturbed annually, they are suppressed as the opportunity to seed onto bare ground diminishes, and perennial and woody species take over.

Also found on urban 'wasteland' are the common perennials such as nettle and couch, which have roots that can survive frequent disturbance, but can also persist in grassland and other undisturbed ground.

'Wasteland' annuals/biennials

Corncockle	*Agrostemma githago*
Scarlet pimpernel	*Anagallis arvensis*
Shepherd's purse	*Capsella bursa pastoris*
Cornflower	*Centaurea cyanus*
Fat-hen	*Chenopodium album*
Corn marigold	*Chrysanthemum segetum*
Red deadnettle	*Lamium purpureum*
Toadflax	*Linaria vulgaris*
Scentless mayweed	*Tripleurospermum inodorum*
Pineapple mayweed	*Matricaria discoidea*
Common poppy	*Papaver rhoeas*
Annual meadow grass	*Poa annua*
Redshank	*Persicaria maculosa*
Weld	*Reseda luteola*
Groundsel	*Senecio vulgaris*
Garlic mustard	*Sisymbrium officinale*
Smooth sowthistle	*Sonchus oleraceus*
Common chickweed	*Stellaria media*
Charlock	*Sinapis arvensis*
Teasel	*Dipsacus fullonum*

'Wasteland' perennials

Couch grass	*Elytrigia repens*
Chicory	*Cichorium intybus*
Creeping thistle	*Cirsium arvense*
Creeping buttercup	*Ranunculus repens*
Coltsfoot	*Tussilago farfara*
Stinging nettle	*Urtica dioica*
White deadnettle	*Lamium album*

In urban areas, many ruderal species may be naturalised species. Some of these are garden escapes, that have been deliberately introduced into Britain to grow in gardens, and then become naturalised on waste ground, spread by wind-borne seeds or birds, or by being dumped as garden refuse. In places these species can become abundant, and waste ground of particular towns become dominated by the locally dominant species, such as buddleia, Michaelmas daisies or evening primrose. Some naturalised species are cultivated hybrid crop plants such as strains of clover. Other naturalised plants become established from seed brought into the country in imported goods, with docks and other handling areas being the focus for these plants to establish.

Naturalised species

Angelica	*Angelica archangelica*
Buddleia	*Buddleia davidii*
Marigold	*Calendula officinalis*
Californian poppy	*Eschscholtzia californica*
Sunflower	*Helianthus annuus*
Poached egg plant	*Limnanthes douglasii*
Honesty	*Lunaria biennis*
Lupin	*Lupinus arboreus*
Night-scented stock	*Matthiola bicornis*

Evening primrose	*Oenothera biennis*
Giant thistle	*Onopordum acanthium*
Opium poppy	*Papaver somniferum*
Oxford ragwort	*Senecio squalidus*
Golden rod	*Solidago canadensis*
Nasturtium	*Tropaeolum majus*
Canary creeper	*Tropaeolum peregrinum*

As described above, urban areas have a significantly warmer climate than surrounding rural areas, allowing southern species to thrive further north than in the countryside. These include both native species, and naturalised aliens.

Urban areas thus have the bare land for plants to establish, the seed source from gardens and imported goods, and the climate for exotics to survive. As described above (p31), some industrial sites also have unusual substrates which support plants typical of salt marsh, sand dune or other habitats, thus increasing the range of the urban flora. For a full discussion of this subject see *The flowering of the cities: the natural flora of urban commons*, English Nature (1992).

In contrast to these recent arrivals are the relict areas of woodland, meadow, wetland and other ancient semi-natural habitat encapsulated in the urban areas, and which contain assemblages of mainly native plants.

FAUNA

The ancient relict areas of semi-natural habitat are especially important for invertebrates, many of which are immobile and require continuity of habitat. These include invertebrates dependent on trees and other plants, dead wood, and those living in the soil. Provided there is continuity of habitat, urban areas can be rich in invertebrates, and even small areas can support significant populations. Warmer temperatures in towns, and the presence of nectar bearing plants over a long season can favour invertebrates. Urban beekeepers are able to produce high volumes of honey because of the good quality, abundant food supply from garden plants.

Recently disturbed sites with areas of bare ground may be good for early stage colonisers such as carabid beetles, and also for solitary ground-nesting bees and wasps. Buddleia and other shrubs may attract stem-nesting bees and wasps. Trampling and grass-mowing are detrimental to the development of the invertebrate community.

Non-native invertebrates possibly comprise 15% of the urban soil invertebrate species, a higher proportion than in rural areas. Most species have little or no effect on the local ecosystem, and have integrated well. The factors in urban areas which encourage the ingress of plant species, also favour invertebrates. These include the importing of goods or plants, the presence of disturbed ground and vacant niches to be exploited, and the means for dispersal along transport corridors. Importing of plants is controlled by plant health regulations, with the aim of preventing the import and spread of pests and diseases. Invertebrate pests are mostly specific to particular ornamental plants and greenhouse crops, and do not cause a problem in the wider environment. However, one particular invertebrate, the New Zealand flatworm, is threatening native earthworm populations in the areas where it has become established. The flatworm is thought to have arrived in this country and spread via the soil in container-grown plants.

Many birds have adapted well to the abundant woodland glade habitat provided by surburban gardens and parks, and 'garden birds' form a major category in a description of the birds of Britain. Garden bird populations increase with suitable nesting cover in overgrown gardens and wilder patches of green space, and with abundant food supplies. These include the insects, berries and fruit of gardens and green spaces, plus additional food put out in bird feeders during the winter. Other birds, particularly those that naturally nest and roost on cliffs, have adapted to city centre living. These include pigeons, herring gulls, swifts, house martins, black redstarts and kestrels. Scavenging species such as the black-headed gull thrive on the food from refuse tips, and starlings have become prolific winter visitors, roosting at night on urban rooftops and feeding by day in parks and fields. Birds of prey, particularly kestrels, are now quite numerous in urban areas, partly due to the abundant food source on motorway and other road embankments. Reservoirs, restored gravel workings, sewage works and other waterways and wetlands within urban areas support abundant populations of resident birds, as well as winter visitors.

Amphibians are able to survive in the wilder green spaces in towns and suburban gardens, provided their habitat is not fragmented and there is safe access to a pond or wetland. Amphibians need fish-free ponds with gently sloping banks, and plenty of cover and foraging habitat nearby. However, populations can be severely reduced by thoughtless actions, such as the cutting of long grass around ponds at the time froglets are emerging. Some drains and other man-made structures can be lethal traps for amphibians, as well as for other animals such as hedgehogs and grass snakes.

Many small mammals are locally abundant in urban areas, and thrive wherever there is suitable cover of long grass, shrubs and other undisturbed vegetation. Several species are good colonisers, able to take advantage of new habitats. Hedgehogs, bats, grey squirrels and weasels are found in many urban areas. Of the larger mammals, foxes have become adept at exploiting the abundant food source in towns, making their earths in railway embankments and waste land. A night-time drive around a town will often include the sighting of a confident-looking fox, quite at home and unworried by car headlights or traffic noise. Rural foxes are much more elusive. In recent years, muntjac deer have spread into suburban habitats, especially in the southern and central Midlands, where they graze on the ground flora in woods and large gardens.

Size and isolation

This section looks at the factors of size and isolation in urban green space. In general, the number of species present on a site increases with increasing site area, but eventually reaches a point where few new species are added. However, various studies suggest that although there is some correlation between species number and the size of urban green space sites, factors other than site size may be equally important. These factors include habitat diversity, management and use, site history, vegetation structure, topography and location.

Small site size is not a problem for most plant species, which do not require a minimum viable area, and the mosaic of many small urban green spaces supports a very wide range of plant species, many of which can disperse to unconnected sites.

Given the right conditions of soil, moisture and climate, many plant species have the potential to survive in urban areas, and have the ability to colonise new areas. Plants with very specific soils needs, such as heather, can survive in small, isolated patches, but will never develop the full range of invertebrate and other fauna supported by large tracts of heathland.

For most animal species, factors other than site size are more important. In general, habitats which combine a varied structure with continuity of management tend to have the highest number of species. For invertebrates of limited mobility, continuity of habitat from year to year is of prime importance, as they find it difficult to move to new sites, and unlike plants, they cannot lie dormant as seeds until conditions become suitable. Small mammals and some invertebrates need long grass and clumps of vegetation which provide cover up to about 500mm above the ground. The presence of the complete range of woodland layers, together with clearings, glades, damp ground and dead wood habitats, tends to maximise the number of bird and invertebrate species. Breeding birds in woodland need dense undisturbed thickets and other refuges.

The urban fauna includes many generalist species, which are those that can thrive on habitat diversity and do not need large areas of habitat. Urban areas cannot hope to support species whose requirements are for large tracts of similar habitat, such as woodland, heathland, rough grassland or wetland, or those species that resent human disturbance.

This suggests that even small green spaces and sites can have some value for wildlife. The aim should be to create a matrix, connecting if possible, of small sites, gardens, hedges, plant-covered walls and roofs, nest boxes and feeding stations. All green spaces are valuable and no opportunity should be passed by to create or preserve them. Even very small areas of relict habitat are of importance and need preserving, if necessary by maintaining existing management to prevent succession. Newly disturbed ground, of however small an area, has potential to develop an interesting flora and fauna, and does not necessarily need management. Larger areas of disturbed ground also have the potential to develop a range of interesting habitats, but requirements of site appearance and use usually dictate intervention. Within large sites, habitat diversity can be produced, which encompasses both continuity and change.

CORRIDORS

Hedgerows, walls, ditches and other linear features can be of wildlife and landscape value, and if primarily required as boundary features, create a bit of 'extra' habitat if constructed and managed sympathetically. Other linear features include roadside verges, railway embankments, canals, riverbanks and strips of woodland, common and meadow land. Their functions as corridors along which species can spread are of varying value. Some plant and animal species are so particular in their requirements that unless precisely the right conditions are present they will not spread. Mobile species tend to be able to move across 'hostile' areas, and corridors have little effect. Linear water features have obvious advantages for the spread of aquatic species and amphibians. Most noticeable, if sometimes unwelcome effects are where introduced species spread rapidly along corridors, particularly road, railway, canal and riversides. Examples include Oxford ragwort, Himalyan balsam, Japanese knotweed, mink, zebra mussel, American crayfish and zander, an Eastern European species of fish now present in the Fens.

The current advice (*Are habitat corridors conduits for animals and plants in a fragmented landscape?*, English Nature, 1994) is that corridors should be preserved, enhanced or created, where cost-effective, as corridors permit certain species to thrive where they otherwise would not. Corridors should be as wide and continuous as possible, with the habitat managed to match the requirements of the target species. However, where resources are limited, alternative measures to conserve biodiversity may have priority.

Corridors along disused railways or linking areas of amenity land are of great value for recreational walking and cycling, which can combine with nature conservation management. Creation and management of corridors in urban areas should perhaps concentrate on this use, for which grant aid and other support may be obtainable.

VERY SMALL SITES

Even very small areas of only a few square metres can be of value, and are worth conserving or creating. In general, existing patches of scrub or groups of trees should be protected, and areas of boggy ground left undrained and kept clear of any encroaching scrub. Rough grass with tussocks can be invaluable for some invertebrates. Small areas with restricted existing wildlife interest can be planted with nectar or berrying perennials and shrubs which provide 'feeding stations' for butterflies and birds. Small ponds attract invertebrates and birds, and with suitable cover nearby can be home to frogs and smooth newts. Small nature gardens, attached to schools, hospitals and old people's homes have particular value because of the use they receive, by those people who may otherwise have little opportunity to experience gardens or wildlife.

These very small areas can be self-contained, useful and viable, but are of much greater wildlife value if they are part of a larger green area, such as a park or school grounds, as there is a greater chance of species being available to benefit from the new habitat created.

MEDIUM-SIZED SITES

These are sites up to about 2 ha in size, and include many school and other institutional grounds, small parks, and types of semi-natural green space described above. Many of these sites have potential for sustaining a variety of habitats and uses which will increase their value for wildlife and community use.

LARGE SITES

These include large areas of woodland, commons and wetlands, which may need some management to improve public access and habitat quality and variety. There are also large areas of wasteland and derelict industrial sites with potential for sympathetic management to retain existing wildlife value, whilst improving appearance, accessibility and value to the community. Many formal urban parks are underused and expensive to maintain by traditional forms of park management, and have potential to include different uses and types of management.

Large sites have their own microclimate, which is significantly different from the surrounding built up areas, having higher humidity, reduced turbulence, and lower temperatures. Larger sites also have a greater capacity to intercept noise and airborne particles, and to absorb water and reduce the rate of run-off. However, as trees have a major role to play in these actions, the amount and type of woodland cover is likely to be more significant that the size of the site.

Site history

The wide variety of urban habitats reflects their past and present use.

RELICT HABITATS

These are areas of land which, for a variety of reasons, have remained relatively untouched by the urban development which surrounds them. This may be due to natural factors such as drainage or topography, which made them unsuitable for building, or due to the type of ownership which has allowed either non-intervention or low levels of management to continue throughout the process of urbanisation.

Common land has been the means by which some habitats have been protected over many centuries. These ancient commons were established for grazing, gathering of fuel and other purposes, for the benefit of those local people with common rights, although usually remaining in the ownership of the lord of the manor. Port Meadow in Oxford, 350 acres in extent, has been an open common since 1086, and Preston Moor since 1253, though it was made into a formal park in 1867. However, particularly in urban areas of the midlands and north, many commons were lost where owners enclosed the land for building. Commons are usually of land which, for reasons of poor soil, were not valued for cultivation. Many are heath, moor, or acid woodland, and through long periods of minimal intervention, have retained much of their natural character and interest.

Areas of ancient semi-natural woodland have survived, for example, in parks, on golf courses and on steep, inaccessible land. Old hedgerows, which may contain descendants of the ancient semi-natural woodland, still survive. Individual trees may be survivors of former woodland, long pre-dating the housing and garden planting now intermingled with them. However, not all old trees are of native origin. Oaks in particular were widely planted during the 17th and 18th Centuries, with much of the planting stock introduced from the continent.

Relict areas of grassland, which have not been fertilised or resown, may occur on commons, water meadows, and in parks, churchyards and golf courses. Other areas of grassland in gardens and recreational sites have been sown or largely altered by management. Some areas of heathland remain, but once fragmented by roads or housing become degraded and of less value for the particular wildlife they support. Great efforts are being put into protecting from development those areas that remain.

River and estuarine habitats are amongst the most natural ecosystems in this country, but in urban areas most have been radically altered for building, transport systems and flood prevention. However, many rivers are less polluted now than they have been for a century or more, and support an increasing range of aquatic and marginal vegetation, fish and other fauna, and where their beds, banks, flood meadows and other features survive in near-natural form, there is increasing interest in protecting them from development.

INDUSTRIAL AND DEVELOPMENT SITES

These include various types of land which have been used in the past for industry, housing or quarrying. Some of these may be vacant in the short-term, awaiting further development, but others are long abandoned sites which would require major restoration to be of use for development. Many support an interesting assemblage of flora and fauna, due to their disturbed soils, extremes of pH, impeded drainage patterns or topography. These may support dynamic, changing habitats, or species which are uncommon. In other cases their physical limitations may act as a brake on natural succession, so maintaining high floral diversity and early succession invertebrates, many of which are uncommon. The inaccessibility of some sites also adds to their wildlife value, supporting species which are intolerant of human disturbance.

Many of these sites comprise tips of various types, including building rubble, pulverised fuel ash (PFA), colliery shale, lime sludge, steel slag, lead mine spoil and jewellers' rouge lagoons produced during plate glass manufacture.

Tips of PFA totalled an area of 1,400 ha in Britain by 1979, of which about 400 ha had been left to colonise naturally. These have produced botanically exciting habitats, ranging from floating fens and bogs to dry woodland. In the initial stages of the succession, the high salt content supports a range of plants typical of coastal sand dunes, which appear even at sites many miles from the sea. The salts are gradually leached out, and between about eight and 20 years after the tip was abandoned a very wide range of plants appear, notably orchids in dense, spectacular stands. These are eventually succeeded by woodland. The constant creation of tips in the past ensured the supply of these dynamic habitats. Ironically, now that coal-powered electricity generation is sharply declining and tipping is brought under greater control, few new sites are being created, and those that remain need protection and management to retain their botanic variety. For further details see Shaw, P (1994).

Old quarries have value for their geological exposures, as well as associated flora and fauna. RIGS (Regionally Important Geological/Geomorphological Sites) are sites that are considered worthy of protection for their educational, research, historical or aesthetic importance. RIGS are selected and conserved at local level by RIGS groups, which may draw their membership from the county wildlife trust, local museum and earth science society, together with local authority representatives and teachers, as well as local minerals industry and landowner associations. RIGS are supported by English Nature and the Geologists' Association, from whom further details are available.

Areas of land awaiting development support interesting ruderal vegetation and associated fauna, and depending on your point of view, can either be seen as exciting wildlife habitats, or neglected areas of wasteland, suggestive of urban decay. In some cities, many of these sites are covered with topsoil, and then sown with quick-growing rye-grass with areas of tree-planting to improve appearance and encourage investment in the area. This type of treatment is expensive, and suppresses the naturally developing wildlife interest. In Sheffield, the practice in recent decades has been to leave the sites to vegetate naturally, and within 3-4 years they support a ruderal vegetation dominated by goat's rue and Michaelmas daisy. These sites are colourful and alive with butterflies, grasshoppers and flocks of seed eating birds during the summer months, but mostly unattractive during the winter. Efforts are being made to find a compromise, which improves the speed of colonisation and the winter appearance of these sites, but retains the spontaneous element. The 6 ha site of a demolished steel works in the Lower Don Valley comprised a mosaic of concrete floors, spreads of rubble and areas of finer material. The margins, entrances and several square shaped areas of fine material were sown with a fescue-dominated mix, and produced bold areas of green which improved the site's appearance. The remaining 35% of the site was left to colonise naturally with the area's spontaneous and spectacular local vegetation. The bold geometric pattern left by the former land use created an exciting and attractive new landscape. For further details see *Enact*, English Nature (vol 3. no 4).

There is a real challenge in choosing the best ways to manage these areas of urban green space to make them visually attractive, of value to wildlife, and accessible and useful to the local people. Many redundant industrial sites are ugly and dangerous, with unstable slopes, unsafe underground workings, steep banked pools, methane leakage and toxic wastes. Restoration is needed to make these sites safe for conservation and amenity use, whilst retaining any features which are, or could be, valuable. Other sites may, in their existing state, have wildlife value, historical interest or particular associations for local people. Through consultation and by taking account of people's knowledge and feelings about the site, 'improvement schemes' which are unnecessary or inappropriate can be avoided.

TRANSPORT NETWORKS

Redundant transport networks include disused railways and canals. Where they are still continuous, they provide valuable green corridors through urban areas. They have value for the wildlife they contain, as corridors along which wildlife can spread, and as traffic-free cycle and walking routes, which can also retain some wildlife value. Most canals with potential for restoration are now back in use for recreational boating, and some sections incorporate towpaths for walking and cycling. Cycleways are likely to be developed along suitable redundant railways and other corridors. Short sections which are no longer continuous can be managed as walks or linear parks, or for cycling, joined with other suitable cycling routes.

Cycleways need careful consultation and design, both to make them safe for cyclists, and to avoid conflict with walkers and local residents. With the National Cycle Network and other cycling initiatives forging ahead, experience and advice in this area is developing rapidly. Detailed information is given in *Making Ways for the Bicycle* (Sustrans, 1994) and *The National Cycle Network: Guidelines and Practical Details Issue 2* (Sustrans, 1997). Contact Sustrans (p133) for details of information leaflets, technical publications and route maps.

Working canals have plenty of opportunities for practical conservation work, in repairs to the canal banks, towpaths, and management of canalside vegetation. For further information contact British Waterways, (p132) and the Waterways Recovery Group (p134).

CHURCHYARDS AND CEMETERIES

Many churchyards and cemeteries are situated on old meadowland or pastures, and are often very rich in plant species. Small rural churchyards of less than an acre may have well over a hundred species of flowering plants, ferns and lichens, as well as an interesting invertebrate fauna. Air pollution, isolation and other factors result in city churchyards and cemeteries having fewer species, but they can still be important habitats within their local area. Churchyards which are either neglected and overgrown, or those which are managed intensively as a garden can both benefit from management which is sensitive to wildlife.

Costs of intensive maintenance can be reduced by introducing a mowing regime which results in a mosaic of differently cut grassland, which will benefit a range of plants and invertebrates. This mosaic could include areas cut every other year, areas cut once a year, areas cut 3-4 times a year, and closely mown paths and lawns. Note that different machines are needed to cut grass of different lengths.

Formal areas of bedding plants or roses can be planted with perennial nectar-producing wild and garden species which will provide food for butterflies and invertebrates from early spring to early autumn. Planting of native shrubs and trees for shelter and shade will also provide food and nesting sites for birds. Nest boxes can be sited around the churchyard, with special boxes for owls and falcons to encourage nesting in the church tower.

Churchyards are of great significance for lichens, and over 300 of the 1700 British species have been found on churchyard stone in lowland England. Almost half the species are rare, being found in only a few sites, and some seldom occur in any other habitat. Rural churchyards in western Britain are particularly notable, but many urban churchyards are also valuable sites. Lichens grow very slowly, and are long-lived, so individual plants on old gravestones may be almost as old as the graves themselves. Lichens need constant conditions of light, and will decline if stones become overgrown or have their orientation changed. They are easily damaged by herbicides. Lichens do not damage the stonework, but protect it from weathering, and should be left to grow unless there is a particular desire to keep all the lettering legible. The roots of mosses can cause damage, especially on statuary, resulting in flaking in frosty weather. The gravestones and other stonework in churchyards are useful for the study of geology, and link well with local history and quarrying.

Churchyard projects can involve many different interest groups, including local historians, geologists, lichenologists, those with a particular interest in birds or butterflies, as well as local parishioners with an interest in gardening or flower arranging. The churchyard can become a focus for human activity as well as wildlife, yet still remain a place of solace and contemplation.

The Church and Conservation Project can provide a range of information on all aspects of nature conservation in churchyards and cemeteries, including leaflets, information packs, audio-visual material and advice on training days. Note that some work, such as the erection of nestboxes or other structures, will require permission from the Diocese.

For further details see Cooper, Nigel, Church House Publishing (1995), and contact The Church and Conservation Project (p132).

DERELICT GARDENS AND ALLOTMENTS

These tend to get overgrown with invasive species such as bramble and elder, which have a high value for some types of wildlife, but may not be the best use where green space is lacking. Where permission from landowners can be gained, the local community may find new ways of managing these areas. Sufficient management to keep paths clear, and provide a variety of habitats for wildlife and informal recreation may be the answer. Old allotments have fertile soils, and it may be possible to revive interest in cultivating them through the approach of permaculture and organic gardening, which has attraction for many people interested in sustainable lifestyles.

RECREATIONAL GREEN SPACE

These include parks, sports grounds, golf courses, and school grounds. Some of these include areas of semi-natural habitat, retained for screening or other purposes, or because their topography makes them unsuitable for recreation. On many sites there is potential for increasing the wildlife value of recreational green space, and also increasing their use as natural green spaces for people to enjoy. Many parks and recreation areas could do with less investment in grass-cutting and herbicides, and greater investment in staff who can manage and help others enjoy more natural landscapes. Sheffield has been leading the way in introducing more natural approaches to park management.

Prestwich Forest Park, Lancashire

This 250 hectare site of derelict and underused land is owned by Bury Metropolitan Council. The site is very variable, with some areas contaminated by heavy metals, lime and other waste materials, but including areas of undisturbed ground.

Since 1991, BTCV has been actively involved in many aspects of management and development on the site. Work has included planting over 25,000 trees, by local residents, school and conservation groups. The planting has been very successful, with few failures even in drought years, and with little maintenance required for the young trees. The success is due to the use of small planting stock, closely spaced. A twenty-year-old plantation has been thinned, and another area of woodland has been set aside for harvesting woodland produce for basket making and wood turning, to encourage interest in the long-term management of the woodlands.

School groups use the site for nature walks, pond dipping and other activities. The educational use is set to greatly increase with the opening of an Environmental Education Centre nearby. In common with many urban sites, Prestwich Forest Park suffers from vandalism, fly-tipping and other problems, which will only be prevented by increased wardening.

Facing Plate 3

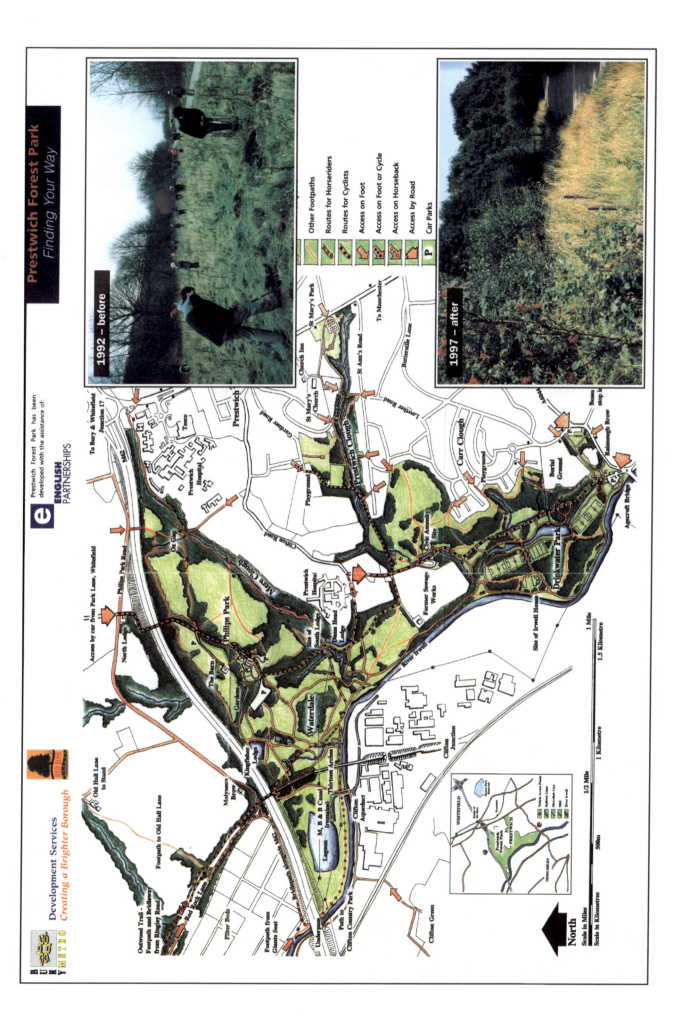

Prestwich Forest Park
Finding Your Way

Prestwich Forest Park has been developed with the assistance of:

ENGLISH PARTNERSHIPS

Development Services
Creating a Brighter Borough

1992 – before

1997 – after

Other Footpaths
Routes for Horseriders
Routes for Cyclists
Access on Foot
Access on Foot or Cycle
Access on Horseback
Access by Road
Car Parks

North

Scale in Miles
Scale in Kilometres

Plate 3

Low Brankin Moor Ecology Park, Darlington

Forest Fields Play Centre Nature Garden, Nottingham

Plate 4

Low Brankin Moor Ecology Park, Darlington

Low Brankin Moor Ecology Park, near Darlington, is a two hectare area of abandoned allotments, enclosed by road, railway and caravan park (see opposite, top left). The area was characterised by thickets of scrub and brambles, interspersed with open glades. BTCV has worked on the site for several years to diversify the range of habitats, in order to increase the value of the area for wildlife, and to create an outdoor classroom for use by local schools. Work has included the planting of broadleaved woodland, the establishment of spring and summer meadows, and the creation of ponds, wetland areas and a butterfly garden.

The existing areas of scrub, bramble and wild roses are very valuable as they provide breeding sites for birds, including whitethroats, blackcaps and garden warblers, and for many small mammals, as well as foraging and hibernation sites for amphibians and invertebrates. The management objective is to maintain the scrub in its present condition by preventing its succession to woodland. This requires the removal of sycamore and other colonising trees. The glades are kept open by mowing or scything at a variety of sward heights, to benefit a diversity of invertebrates. The scrub habitat is vulnerable to being destroyed by vandals who start fires.

A wide variety of native broadleaved trees have been planted to create a diverse woodland, with the aim of attracting invertebrates. The fertile soil of the former allotments is a hindrance in the formation of a woodland flora, as it favours the growth of grasses, and it will be some years before the trees cast sufficient shade to allow woodland species to compete. For the first few years after planting the grass was cut and removed during the summer, to prevent it physically smothering the young trees. Ramsons, bluebell and wood anemone have been planted. Understorey shrubs such as rose species are retained, but cut back where they are smothering young trees. Young Scots pine are pruned of their lower branches, to reduce their appeal as potential Christmas trees.

A spring meadow has been sown with plants that flower and set seed early in the year. The sward is cut in July, after the seeding of annual plants such as the yellow rattle, and before the coarser grasses have set seed. The cuttings are left on the meadow for two days to allow the seeds to fall, and are then removed from the meadow and scattered in the scrub areas. For the remainder of the growing season, the sward is kept at a height of no more than 5cm, and the cuttings removed. While cutting, aggressive use of mechanical scrubcutters creates areas of bare earth in which herb seeds can germinate.

Two ponds have been dug, one large and shallow, the other smaller and deeper, with a drainage ditch running between them. A path alongside is kept close-mown all year, to encourage access only to one side of the ponds, leaving the other sides undisturbed for amphibians and invertebrates. All management work is also carried out from the path. A large stand of reedmace is kept to a maximum area of four square metres, to prevent it invading the entire pond. Other pond vegetation is removed in rotation, no more than one-fifth being cleared each year.

Forest Fields Play Centre Nature Garden, Nottingham

Forest Fields Play Centre Nature Garden, Nottingham, was created in a part of the playground attached to the Play Centre, which is in a heavily built up area of the city. The Play Centre is a place for local children, aged 5-14, to go after school and in the holidays. BTCV worked with the playleaders to design and construct a small pond, bog and raised beds in an area of about 30 sq metres, with the aim of introducing the children to wildlife gardening and environmental issues, and of providing an area for practical activity through the seasons.

The main practical work was done over two days. This included removing a redundant fence of concrete sleepers, which were re-used to make the raised beds, creating a small pond using a triple-bonded PVC liner, and building a small rockery. Some of the staff and children then visited a local garden centre to choose the native plants for the raised beds, pond and bog, which the children helped plant. Plants included 36 species of marginals, deep water oxygenating plants, heathers for an 'acid' bed, about 25 native flowering plants, with shrubs and climbers for the walls and fences. The materials and plants for the nature garden totalled £916, and the project was grant-aided by English Nature.

The children greatly enjoyed helping create the garden, and it has provided a focus for other activities such as raising plants from seed. The garden gives a much needed greener, quieter corner for the children to enjoy, separated by a fence from the hurly-burly of the playground. Frog and toad spawn are being introduced into the pond, and hopefully some butterflies and other invertebrates will be attracted to the garden. The play centre is surrounded by terraced housing with small walled yards, but very little greenery. There is great potential for improving the environment with further native and garden planting, and the greatest benefit would be if the play centre garden provided the inspiration for local families to follow.

Craigton Cemetery, Glasgow

Craigton Cemetery is a 22 hectare cemetery on the southern outskirts of Glasgow. The site is privately owned, and over the years has been neglected, with fly-tipping and litter, vandalism and the invasive growth of Japanese knotweed. Although some of the lack of management has been beneficial for wildlife, with growth of trees, shrubs and other native plants, the general appearance is of neglect, which causes further problems of vandalism, as well as distress to relatives visiting the site.

EAGER became involved with the site, and a management plan was drawn up to concentrate the limited resources available on improving the appearance of the most visible parts of the cemetery. The remainder of the site would receive lower maintenance, thus maintaining the wildlife value, whilst improving the paths to encourage public use of the site for walking and quiet recreation.

The main objectives were the following:

- Removal of all rubbish from the site. After the initial clean-up, rubbish removal from verges and visible areas to remain the priority task of every visit to the site, with additional visits to specifically clear rubbish from elsewhere on the site.

- Removal of accumulated cut woody material by chipping. Further cuttings and prunings from site management work to be chipped in order to prevent accumulation in the future. Chippings to be used for path surfacing or mulch.

- The verge of the entrance road to be improved by mowing, and wooden posts to be installed to prevent cars parking on the verges and churning them up.

- Repair of fencing.

- Removal of Japanese knotweed by herbicide spray.

- Hedge and tree planting.

Field study trips have been made to the cemetery by local school groups, and volunteers have helped with planting of bulbs and wildflowers.

Beersbridge Nature Walk, Belfast

Beersbridge Nature Walk, Belfast, has been created on a section of redundant railway which had become a site for fly-tipping and other unsocial activities. Conservation Volunteers Northern Ireland have been involved in making many improvements to the site, including removal of rubbish, path surfacing, fencing and vegetation management, which has transformed the site into a popular, attractive path used by hundreds of people every day. These include blind people with guide dogs, from a nearby centre for the blind, and this has led to the production of a taped guided walk, with funding from the Sensory Trust. Walkmans or big print guide books are used, referenced to brightly coloured posts for those with a little vision. A tactile map is also being produced.

Captain's Clough, Bolton

Captain's Clough, in the heart of Bolton, is a beautiful wooded valley which had been neglected for many years. Local people, in partnership with Bolton Metro Council, Bolton Wildlife Project and BTCV, have transformed the site from a derelict, fly-tipped area into an open space which the whole community can enjoy. The focus of the project is a new footpath which makes the valley accessible to everyone and, as the site is right on the residents' doorsteps, has been an important element in involving as many people in the project as possible.

Craigton Cemetery, Glasgow

Beersbridge Nature Walk, Belfast – before

After

Captain's Clough, Bolton

Plate 5

5   Siteworks

Rubbish, debris and artifacts

Clearing rubbish, removing burnt out cars and preventing fly-tipping has been the catalyst to practical action on many urban sites. Removing the remains of derelict buildings, fences, areas of concrete and so on may also be desirable for aesthetic reasons, or to make way for habitat creation, community gardens or other projects. Rubbish and debris does have its benefits for wildlife (p12), and industrial dereliction has many interesting ecological effects (p36), as well as having local history value. Sweeping away all evidence of man's activity may not be the best approach, but for most people, removing the obvious evidence of fly- tipping and dereliction is an essential starting point to discourage further misuse of the site and to raise the profile of the area for local residents. Unacceptable refuse which is valuable for wildlife can be replaced by more acceptable substitutes such as 'habitat piles' of stones or timber, compost heaps, and dry stone walls and banks. Common ivy and other climbing plants can be planted to hide unsightly debris, at the same time as providing flowers, fruit and shelter for many organisms. Purpose-built animal homes can also be provided (see chapter 10).

Rubbish provides winter hibernation sites for small mammals and amphibians, and nesting sites for many animals from March to October. Clearance of rubbish of all types is best done in early autumn, before hibernation.

For publicity purposes, take 'before' and 'after' photos, and keep a record of the number of bags or skips filled.

HAZARDOUS WASTE

Prior to work starting, the site should be checked by the project leader or site manager for any hazardous rubbish or debris. This might include chemicals, asbestos, medical waste, or other items. Contact the local office of the Environment Agency for advice if such items are found. Burnt-out and derelict cars have a range of serious hazards associated with them, and should be removed by licensed scrap dealers (see below). Any hazardous material or derelict cars that are not removed should be fenced off and marked, as should any that are uncovered during the course of work. If chemical leakage or a possibility of explosion is detected, then work should cease on the site.

NON-HAZARDOUS WASTE

Most people will see little beauty or benefit in rubbish or derelict buildings. However, some materials can be re-used on the site and many materials can be reclaimed. Check at your local waste disposal site about which materials they reclaim, so that materials can be sorted into different categories as you collect them.

Metal waste of all types can be collected for recycling. Before clearance work starts, try and estimate the amount of metal waste and have sufficient skips ready for collecting, to save handling it more than once. Prices will vary, but often scrap-metal collection can prove a worthwhile money-raising venture in its own right. Some scrap-metal merchants will deliver and collect their own skips. Check your local Yellow Pages for the best deal.

Metal waste can provide hibernation and nesting sites, especially when overgrown with bramble, ivy and other plants. Depending on the future use of the site, it may be best to leave the material in situ if it is already well grown over. Other metal material can be left to grow over if it is out of public view, and is likely to be left 'unvandalised' for long enough for it to become a useful habitat.

Large metal items that are not dangerous can be left as 'vandal honeypots' (p29). If they are moveable and there is an option for siting them, choose somewhere away from any features you wish to protect, sufficiently hidden that they do not constitute an eyesore, but accessible for children. With a bit of luck they will become a place for children to play or vandals to try and wreck, and keep them away from the places you want to protect.

Dumped furniture, old sofas, mattresses and other items are not usually worth reclaiming and should be put in a skip with general rubbish. Metal household items can be recycled. Plastic materials should be removed for disposal or recycling.

Items that are mainly wood can be left to rot down and provide dead wood habitat. In areas where anything made of wood is likely to be set on fire, some of the wood can be partly or completely buried, where it will form a valuable underground habitat for invertebrates and hibernating amphibians. Where this is impractical, remove wood off the site to prevent arson.

Provide sufficient skips at the site to remove the day's collection of rubbish, and if possible arrange for the skips to be collected at the end of the day. Avoid leaving piles of material or full skips which may be sorted over or scattered by the next morning. The carriage and disposal of waste is covered by the Environmental Protection Act 1990, although most voluntary activities are exempt. It would be advisable to check that any skip company used is registered to transport the waste you may generate.

Give a safety talk at the beginning of the day, and demonstrate the proper way of lifting heavy materials. Everyone should wear workgloves and suitable clothing. Wheelbarrows and winches may be needed for moving heavy items. Provide rubbish sacks and litter pickers for smaller items.

Clearance of large, heavy items will need JCBs, skid-steer loaders or dumpers. They must be driven only by trained and competent operators. Position skips to take advantage of any walls or banks which give easy access. Scaffold planks can be used to make a barrow run up to small skips. A pick up truck or trailer is useful for reaching larger skips. For clearance work of large heavy items a JCB or loader will be needed for loading items into the skip.

FLY-TIPPING AND ABANDONED CARS

All UK waste is subject to strict controls, and apart from disposal of household waste in your own garden, waste can only be deposited, recovered or disposed of by operators licensed by the local authority.

Fly-tipping is the dumping of domestic or commercial waste on unauthorised sites, usually from a vehicle. It is illegal, and is covered under the Environmental Protection Act 1990. Anyone fly-tipping is liable to a fine of up to £20,000, or an unlimited amount if indicted to the Crown Court, or an offender can be sent to prison. It is also an offence to permit fly-tipping. The person controlling the use of the vehicle can also be prosecuted, which makes it possible for a prosecution to take place when only the vehicle, not the driver, can be identified. The police have powers to seize vehicles used for fly-tipping.

Newly-abandoned cars should be reported to the police. They or the local authority have the powers to remove abandoned cars, and charge the cost to owners, if they can be traced. Some scrap-metal merchants will remove cars that are accessible by a recovery vehicle, with the scrap value of the car usually balancing the cost of removal.

Fly-tipping and dumping of stolen and abandoned cars can be greatly reduced if vehicle access to the site can be prevented. The status of any rights of way which give access should be checked with the rights of way officer at the local authority. Vehicle access to paths that are bridleways or footpaths can be discouraged with bridle gates or stiles, although on some sites these may be vandalised. Large boulders, bollards or dry ditches may be more effective in stopping vehicle access, although other rights of access must not be infringed.

ARTIFACTS

Abandoned buildings, hard standings and other man-made features can be viewed as industrial heritage or dereliction, according to your point of view and your understanding of the site. Through the local press or by asking around, try and get in touch with people who worked on the site, or have knowledge passed down from previous generations. Such inquiries can generate an interest in a community's roots, and prevent wholesale destruction of past activities.

The surroundings also have a great influence. A derelict building on a derelict site may have little appeal, but could be transformed to an interesting ruin in a wildlife garden.

Safety is an important consideration when deciding what to do with redundant buildings and other artifacts. Demolishing is the usual course of action, to tidy the site, avoid potential dangers, and to prevent buildings attracting anti-social activities. Demolition of any structure is covered by the Construction (Design and Management) Regulations. If anyone is employed to carry out demolition work, advice should be sought from the local office of the Health and Safety Executive. Remaining walls that are low enough not to present a danger can be retained. As well as local history interest, old walls provide habitats for lichens, mosses and climbing plants, and create conditions of shade and damp, shelter and warmth. The wildlife value of the wall will depend on its construction, and the state of the mortar; cavity walls with soft mortar being more habitable than very sound walls.

Building rubble of all types can usually be re-used on site, and should be viewed as a potential bonus rather than a problem. Piles of rubble are perfect hibernation and nesting habitats for all sorts of animals, and will soon become partly grown over and disguised by vegetation. Rubble can be re-used for building walls within the site to delineate different areas and as wildlife habitats. Building rubble is a magnet for children, and as long as it is not dangerous to climb on can be left as a 'honeypot' feature. However, it may need to be removed if its use as a source of missiles could endanger any passers-by or property.

Hard standings of concrete are also part of the site's history, and some may be worth retaining for this reason alone. With time, plants germinate in cracks, and spread in from the edges, and in sunny weather, the warmth of the concrete may attract basking invertebrates or reptiles. Plant growth can be encouraged by cracking the concrete.

Broken up concrete can be used for habitat piles and walls. Concrete crushed into smaller pieces can be rotavated into the subsoil to make a good free draining substrate for supporting flower rich meadows (p85).

Coarse gravel, brick rubble and spreads of other free draining material are in effect like mountain screes, fixed dunes or stony beaches, and like them, support interesting plant communities. A Sheffield site (p37) benefited from a technique to combine these spontaneous communities with more managed and conventionally green areas.

UNDERGROUND AND OVERHEAD SERVICES

These include electricity, gas, water and telecommunications. It should be assumed that all urban sites have underground services until proven otherwise. Initially inspect the site for overhead services, and for the likelihood of underground services if the planned work includes disturbing the ground. Then contact each of the utilities and the local authority to obtain current and complete plans of the depth and location of services. However, underground services plans are notoriously unreliable in their fine detail, as cables and pipes may 'snake' between points, or they may have been moved during subsequent work, or the plan itself may be only a large scale overall guide. If problems are indicated, request that the utilities trace the services accurately with a cable and pipe locating device. To do it yourself, devices can be hired that trace live electricity cables, metal pipes and plastic pipes with a metal tracer laid with them, and water pipes to which you have access at either end. Training is necessary for their use, and it is recommended that you take specialist advice as required.

Having located and marked the line of services, prohibit any digging or ground penetration work within 0.5 metres of the line, and any such work using power tools and mechanical excavators within 1 metre of the line.

For overhead cables, avoid working on trees or other structures within 3 metres of any cables. Plan work to prevent tools, people, vehicles and their attachments or other materials coming within 3 metres of overhead cables.

For further details see *Avoiding danger from underground services*, HS(G)47, Health and Safety Executive (1989).

Access

DESIRE LINES

Many urban sites will already be in use for informal recreation, with existing paths following desire lines across the site, or to particular points of interest. These are nearly always worth retaining, and should not be changed without very good reason. Use them to give the basic framework for access around the site, and fit in any tree planting or habitat creation projects around them. To encourage use and avoid fear of crime, access routes should have open margins of grass or short vegetation. Do not plant shrubs or trees right up to the edges of the path. Guidance on path widths is given below.

Areas sensitive to trampling or human disturbance may need protecting, so avoid routing any new paths near them, or upgrading or publicising any existing paths. Once created, paths are very difficult to get rid of, because

use has become established, and regular users of the site, especially dog walkers and playing children will want to keep using familiar paths. This effect can be put to good use in keeping people away from sensitive areas. For example, once children are used to a particular tunnel through scrub into a favourite den, they are less likely to go exploring elsewhere.

For information on paths in woodland, see chapter 6.

ACCESSIBILITY

The terms 'access' and 'accessibility' are defined as follows (Harrison et al, English Nature, 1995). 'Access refers to certain rights of approach, entry or use that are legally or conventionally defined; accessibility refers to the extent to which these rights can be exercised in particular places, at particular times and by particular people. Determining whether or not natural places are accessible therefore involves thinking not only about site ownership and access rights but also of physical and social considerations which constrain the extent to which access rights can be exercised'.

Any site designed for public use should have at least a part which is accessible to disabled people, elderly, wheelchair users and parents with pushchairs. It is not realistic or desirable to make all areas, regardless of topography, accessible to everyone, but there should be no artificial barriers which restrict access to legitimate users in otherwise suitable areas. On large sites, or in hilly areas, concentrate on improving accessibility to the flatter areas, those nearest housing, car parks or bus stops, and through routes, circular paths, or those linking points of interest. Accessibility is also affected by factors outside the site. For example, a busy road may make a site inaccessible to the old or young, or a steep slope or high kerb outside the site may cause problems for some users.

The most popular paths should be wide with smooth, durable surfacing, to make them attractive and inviting to all. Disabled and other vulnerable groups are most likely to make use of places which are cared for, welcoming, well-used and free from concerns of crime or unsocial activities, which are factors affecting all users.

Particular provisions for the disabled, such as tactile trails or tapping rails for the blind need careful planning if they are going to be successful. Before starting any project, make contact with local day centres, residential homes or other groups who may be interested in using the site. The most successful and well-used projects for improving accessibility for the disabled, visually impaired or deaf are those that have been designed in close co-operation with a nearby user group. The Beersbridge Nature Walk, Belfast (p40) is close to a centre for blind people, who helped design, and frequently use, the special facilities on the Walk. The tactile and musical trails in Barnsley (p16) are sited in the grounds of a riding centre for the disabled.

PATH SPECIFICATON FOR WHEELCHAIR USE

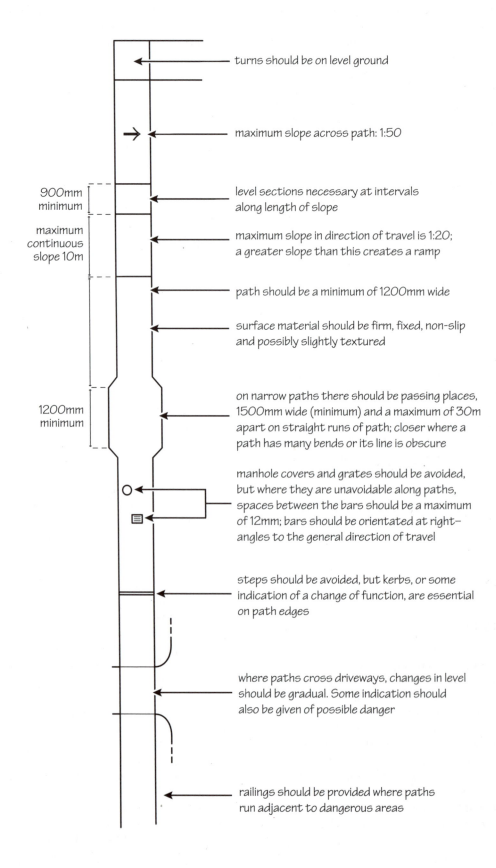

turns should be on level ground

maximum slope across path: 1:50

900mm minimum

level sections necessary at intervals along length of slope

maximum continuous slope 10m

maximum slope in direction of travel is 1:20; a greater slope than this creates a ramp

path should be a minimum of 1200mm wide

surface material should be firm, fixed, non-slip and possibly slightly textured

1200mm minimum

on narrow paths there should be passing places, 1500mm wide (minimum) and a maximum of 30m apart on straight runs of path; closer where a path has many bends or its line is obscure

manhole covers and grates should be avoided, but where they are unavoidable along paths, spaces between the bars should be a maximum of 12mm; bars should be orientated at right–angles to the general direction of travel

steps should be avoided, but kerbs, or some indication of a change of function, are essential on path edges

where paths cross driveways, changes in level should be gradual. Some indication should also be given of possible danger

railings should be provided where paths run adjacent to dangerous areas

Source: Informal countryside recreation for disabled people.
Countryside Commission, 1994

In summary, general upgrading of access provision in popular locations will benefit many users. Specific facilities should be carefully designed in consultation with particular user groups.

Local advice should also be available through disability access officers from the local authority. Advice is available nationally from The Fieldfare Trust. For detailed advice see *Guidelines: A Good Practice Guide to Disabled People's Access in the Countryside*, Fieldfare Trust (1997).

Gradients

The easiest access is along flat or gentle gradients up to a maximum of 1:20 along the path. For wheelchair use, sections of 1:20 should be no more than 10m long, broken with flat sections of at least 900mm length. Maximum slope across the path should be 1:50, with turns made on level ground.

Moderately easy access is given by paths with sections of gentle to moderately steep gradient of between 1:15 and 1:12, and of a smooth hard surface. Long lengths of path with a gradient steeper than 1:12 are difficult for the ambulant disabled.

Ramps

Ramps should be provided as an alternative to steps, but not as a substitute. Many ambulant disabled people with problems of balance find ramps much more difficult than steps. Both ramps and steps may need handrails (see below). Ramps and steps should be a minimum of 1.2m wide, and 1.7m wide for busy areas.

Length of ramp	<3m	3-6m	6m+
Ambulant disabled	1:90	1:12	1:12
Independent wheelchair user	1:10	1:12	1:20
Wheelchair pushed by carer	1:90	1:12	1:20
Electric wheelchair	1:16	1:16	1:20

From *Informal Countryside Recreation for Disabled People*, Countryside Commission (1994).

On long ramps a rest platform should be provided at a maximum of 10m or after each 800mm of vertical rise. The length of rest platforms should not be greater than 1.8m. A level distance of 1.8m continuing in the direction of the ramp should be allowed at the top and bottom to give room for turning.

Slightly roughened surfaces such as brushed concrete give the best grip.

Path width

Selected popular paths should be sufficiently wide for wheelchair and other disabled use. A width of 1.2m is the minimum for wheelchair use, with 1.7m allowing two wheelchairs to pass, or walkers to comfortably pass a wheelchair user. Some elderly walkers, the visually impaired or disabled walkers need the support of an able person beside them, and like to feel they are not holding up other walkers behind them. All users are likely to feel more comfortable and less threatened on a wide path with unenclosed edges. Family and other groups are more likely to use paths where there is room to walk side by side.

Where revetment on slopes, surfacing or other construction is necessary, costs may rise with increasing path width. However, it is not usually sensible to cut costs by reducing path width. If construction or surfacing is considered necessary, at least side by side or two-way pedestrian use should be provided for, which means a minimum width of 1.2m. Where the site is suitable and resources are available, a path of 2m will not seem too wide. This is the width of a rural cart-track, feels comfortable and inviting for family groups and others to walk, and allows a range

PATH WIDTHS

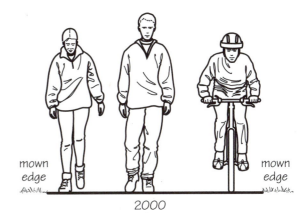

2000
minimum width for shared pedestrian and cycle use – see note in text

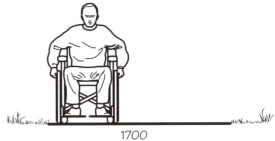

1700
two-way wheelchair, pushchair and pedestrian use

1200
two-way pedestrian use

600
one way pedestrian use

of uses. Wider paths also allow machine construction, which is very much quicker than using manual labour. It may be cost-effective to use a machine to make a wider path, rather than using voluntary labour to construct a narrower path. Some sites will have their own sources of hard-core, subsoil or other material which, with suitable machinery, can be used for path construction. Reclaimed road surfacing material may be available cheaply (p47). Once construction is complete, vehicle use can be prevented by barriers at entrance points.

The treatment of the path edges is important. Where the site is suitable and the maintenance funds available, mown grass is the best option. This itself produces a reasonably hard-wearing surface which can be used as an overspill. It also keeps sight lines open so reducing fear of crime, and prevents loss of path width due to encroaching vegetation. Keep shrub, hedge and tree planting well back from the path, leaving an edge of at least 2m. Any nearer than this,

and frequent pruning will be needed.

The diagram on the previous page shows some of the recommended widths for pedestrian, wheelchair and cycle use. Note that shared pedestrian and cycle use on a 2m width path is only suitable where cycle use is light and overspill onto the verge is possible. Signs or a 'white line' will be needed to indicate which side cyclists must keep to. Most paths for shared cycle and pedestrian use should be at least 3m wide. For full details see *The National Cycle Network: Guidelines and Practical Details Issue 2*, Sustrans (1997).

Surfacing

Smooth, firm and non-slip surfaces are the easiest for all users. Tarmac or concrete are the usual path surfaces in parks and recreation areas, but will detract from the appearance and feel of less intensively managed areas.

SUSTRANS PATH SPECIFICATIONS

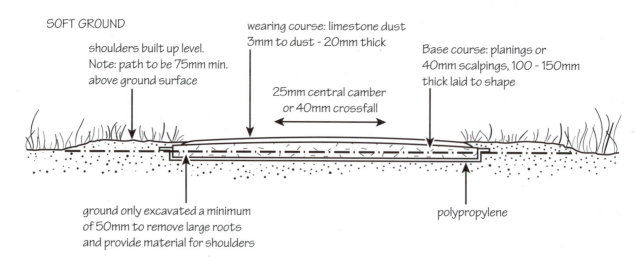

SOFT GROUND

shoulders built up level. Note: path to be 75mm min. above ground surface

wearing course: limestone dust 3mm to dust - 20mm thick

Base course: planings or 40mm scalpings, 100 - 150mm thick laid to shape

25mm central camber or 40mm crossfall

ground only excavated a minimum of 50mm to remove large roots and provide material for shoulders

polypropylene

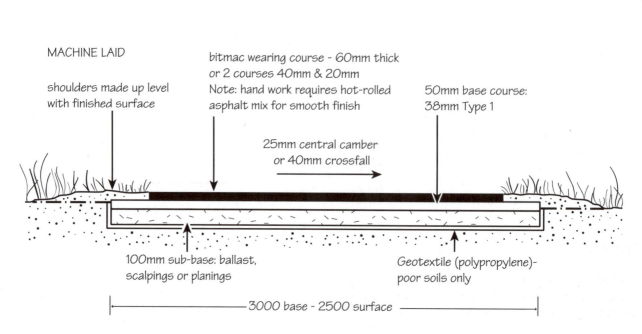

MACHINE LAID

shoulders made up level with finished surface

bitmac wearing course - 60mm thick or 2 courses 40mm & 20mm Note: hand work requires hot-rolled asphalt mix for smooth finish

50mm base course: 38mm Type 1

25mm central camber or 40mm crossfall

100mm sub-base: ballast, scalpings or planings

Geotextile (polypropylene)- poor soils only

3000 base - 2500 surface

Various loose surfacings such as hoggin, crushed stone, planings or scalpings (recovered road surfacing) can be used, firmly compacted with a powered roller or vibrating plate. The material should be gently cambered for drainage. The specification above is recommended by Sustrans, and has been successfully used on many miles of tracks built for cyclists, wheelchair users and walkers.

Information on particular tactile surfaces for visually impaired walkers can be obtained from the RNIB, and Disabled Living Foundation.

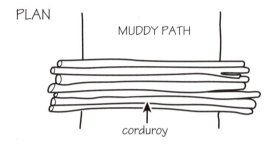

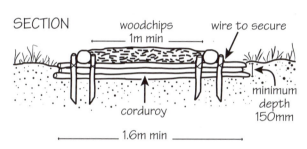

The Woodscape project in Huddersfield (see also page 80) originated from a small group of local dog walkers, who wanted to clear rubbish and improve the access to local woodland. Of the many improvements made, one of the most important is a path about one kilometre long, which links two areas of housing. A mini-digger was hired to clear the route, and excavate a path foundation about 75mm deep. Piped cross drains were installed as necessary, and then about 50 tons of road planings were obtained cheaply and used to surface the path. This recycled material packs down to make an excellent path surface, which in spite of its origin, blends in well with the natural surroundings. The path is popular with many local users, including school children who now use the path to cycle to school, instead of having to go on the school bus.

Other paths through the woods are surfaced as necessary with woodchips, produced from thinning and clearance operations. The layer of woodchips, about 100mm thick, is contained by poles of a similar diameter, secured to the ground with wooden pegs and wires. Where the ground is wet, the woodchips can be laid on a base of 'corduroy', made of poles laid in a closely-packed layer across the path. Poles of diameter from 30-100mm can be used, depending on what is available. A minimum depth of about 150mm is needed, increasing across wetter ground. Woodchip paths need topping up periodically as the material compacts.

Steps

Steps should be at least 1.2m wide, or 1.7m for popular paths. The steps should have a uniform riser height of not more than 170mm, with treads of no less than 250mm, and of uniform size if possible. Avoid variable tread depth by extending the slope and lowering the gradient of the flight of steps. Flights can be separated with landings. Avoid constructions which include open tread or pronounced nosings, which can cause people to trip. Risers of a pale or distinctive colour are easier to see. Avoid single steps, as they are often not noticed.

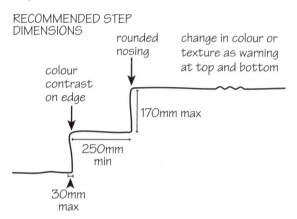

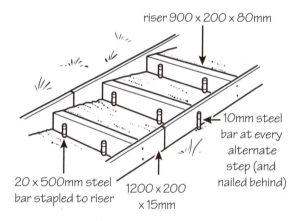

A flight of wooden steps can be built as shown, with edging boards to help contain the surfacing material, which should be hard-packed hoggin or gravel with sufficient clay content to bind together. Surfacing will need replacing periodically. Steps which follow a curving line cannot have an edging board, and will need regular maintenance to keep the step surface in good condition.

Lengths of steel bar make effective 'stobs' to hold the steps in place, and are easier to knock in straight than wooden stobs. Stobs of steel bar can also be of a much smaller diameter than wooden stobs, and can be fitted neatly against the step where they do not present a hazard. Most wooden steps will require maintenance, and in some locations it may be more satisfactory to use stone, brick or concrete for durability. See *Footpaths*, BTCV (1996) for further information.

Brick and slab steps can be constructed as shown. If the bank is of loose soil or other material, you may need to dig out a large area and backfill with hardcore as you build the steps. In firm soil, you need only cut out the rough shape of each step, as shown below. Start by laying the base of hardcore with a concrete foundation about 100mm deep and twice the width of the riser. Then build up the brick risers and slab steps, mortaring all joints.

BRICK AND SLAB STEPS

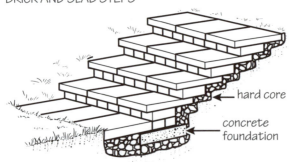

hard core

concrete foundation

To build a small flight of concrete steps, start by casting a foundation slab. Then build up the formwork as shown. The bevel at the front of each step stops the edge crumbling, and the bevel at the bottom of the riser allows the float to pass over the whole surface of the tread during finishing. Set steel rod reinforcing across each step. Roughened or corrugated treads prevent the steps from becoming slippery.

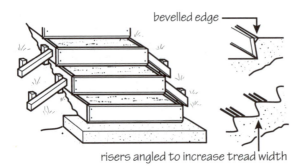

bevelled edge

risers angled to increase tread width

Kerbs

Dropped kerbs to pavements should be provided at any point where wheelchair access may be needed. Dropped kerbs are also needed near gulley pots which are in the vicinity of amphibia breeding pools. A vertical kerb acts as a deflector and channels animals into the gulley pot, where they die.

Handrails

Handrails are needed either to help disabled people up steps or gradients, or as protection against steep drops or other pathside dangers.

Handrails are needed on steps, or ramps of 1:16 or steeper and more than 3m long, in locations which are accessible for elderly or disabled people. The handrail should be

1m vertically above the incline or the nosings of the steps, round or oval in section and 40-50mm in diameter horizontally for easy grip. The rail should extend 300-400mm beyond the end of the incline at the top and the bottom. The rail should be capable of supporting a weight of 90kg. Wheelchair users and children need a rail 750-800mm high. A bottom rail no more than 100mm above the ground is a useful edging for wheelchair users and tapping rail for the visually impaired.

Safety handrails on bridges or above drops should be 1m high, or 1.4m for particularly hazardous situations. A middle rail at 800mm, suitable for grip support, and bottom rail at no more than 100mm above ground must also be fitted. Wire mesh should be fitted on sites where young children may have unsupervised access.

Boardwalks and bridges

The minimum width should be 1.2m for one way use, or 1.7m for two way use. Alternatively, passing places can be provided. Access onto the bridge or boardwalk should be ramped at no more than 1:12 gradient. The decking should be fitted cross-wise, with gaps of 10-16mm. Boardwalks or bridges without handrails should have a toe rail 100mm high. Where required, safety rails of the dimensions given above should be fitted.

In open, sunny situations, boardwalk decking will not become slippery. In shady, damp woodlands where algal growth makes surfaces slippery, epoxy tar sprays with grit can be applied by specialist operators. Alternatively, expanded metal or hexagonal mesh can be attached with staples to give a non-slip surface. This also discourages vandals from removing the decking. Grip can be improved on ramps by fitting strips of hardwood or metal at intervals across the ramp.

As with any artificial structure, boardwalks and bridges must be checked regularly to ensure they are safe for the use for which they are intended.

For further information see *Footpaths*, BTCV (1996).

Seating

Provision of seating needs careful thought. In supervised sites or those attached to day centres, outdoor classrooms or buildings, seats and other outdoor furniture are a useful addition. Seats and rests are appreciated by disabled or elderly, and may make accessible a walk that would otherwise be too tiring. However, seats often become a focus for unsocial activities, attract litter and are subject to vandalism.

On sites that are not supervised, seats are best placed in open locations, overlooked from buildings or roads, but not so near to housing that their use causes problems for

HANDRAIL DIMENSIONS

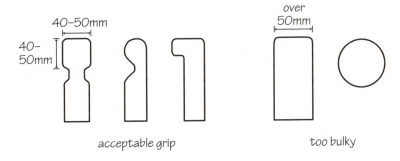

acceptable grip   too bulky

SUPPORT HANDRAILS

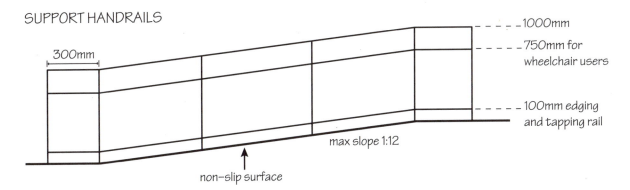

local residents. In particular, seats tend to be a meeting place for young people, and may either fulfil a useful social role, or be a focus for unsocial behaviour. Even a fairly well-behaved group of youths may appear threatening, and can be enough to discourage others from walking past or using the site.

Avoid 'cul-de-sacs' or sites surrounded by bushes or trees. The best sites for sitting, sunny, open and with an interesting view, are also the safest. Two or three seats grouped together, spaced sufficiently to be comfortably occupied by people who don't know each other, but near enough to give security in numbers, are probably better than scattered seats out of view of each other. 'Perches' or rests can be provided at intervals for people who need them, but which are not comfortable enough to encourage others to linger.

Seats or other furniture which attracts unsocial activities should be removed, to break the pattern of behaviour.

SEATS AND BENCHES

Seating can be informal and low cost, using logs, timber and other materials available cheaply or from the site itself. These will have a limited life, are difficult to secure against vandalism, and may be unsuitable for use by disabled or elderly infirm people, who may need armrests to help them up to a standing position.

Seats of stone, brick or concrete should be durable and secure against vandalism, but only build them in sites where you are fairly sure they will not attract unsocial

behaviour, or you will only have the job of later demolishing them.

Low walls and banks can be adapted into seating by topping with flat stones or timber. Very large blocks of stone have been used on some sites to deter vehicle access, and these may be used as informal seats.

A large range of seats and park benches are available from suppliers of park and outdoor furniture. They are mostly well-designed, durable, comfortable but expensive, and need to be secured into concrete bases for security. They are a good investment for supervised sites where they will have frequent use, especially by elderly or disabled who will appreciate their comfort and the provision of arm rests, to ease getting up from the sitting position.

Constructing a simple seat or bench is a useful project in its own right, and one which most people will feel able to tackle. Various designs are shown below. Arm rests are more difficult to fit securely, and if these are thought necessary, the location is likely to be one which will merit the purchase of a commercial product.

Seats should be 450-500mm high, with a top that is either free draining, or constructed with a slight slope to shed water. There should be a heel space of at least 100mm beneath the seat to make it easier to rise from the sitting position. Tops need to be securely fitted to supports or bases, which themselves need to be either very heavy, or secured to the ground. Timber should be free of splinters. Hardwood is best.

Various types of reclaimed materials can be used. Reclaimed timber from building demolition or refurbishment is available from scrapyards. Smaller size pieces of hardwood can be used for slatted timber benching, or larger pieces used as a single slab. Scrap furniture can yield quite large pieces of hardwood, which can be adapted in various ways.

The bench top can be attached to a timber frame, set well into the ground. 100mm square fence posts of preserved softwood are suitable, as they are easy to cut and join to make strong secure joints. Timber supports should be set about 500mm into the ground, in concrete. Bench tops can be secured to timber supports by hardwood dowels, glued into drilled holes, which are more difficult to remove that metal fixings. Thick galvanised wire can be stapled into routered grooves along timbers and over joints to deter saw-bearing vandals or thieves.

Wooden seats around trees are always popular and give a shady place to sit in summer, but without feeling enclosed, and make a virtue out of 'lollipop' trees in mown grass. A big low seat will look more attractive than a small, higher one, and can double as a table or something for children to climb on. Don't attach the seat structure to the tree, and leave at least 75mm space to allow for the trunk to grow.

TREE SEAT

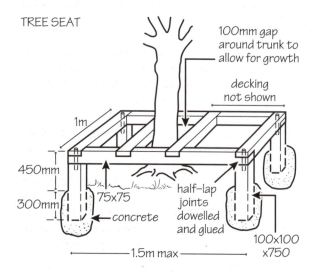

Most sites will yield a supply of bricks, blocks or stones which can be mortared into position to make bench supports for slatted or solid wood tops. The seating can either be set into the supports from the side, or bolted through from the top. A disadvantage of setting them in is that they are difficult to replace if vandalised.

Cast concrete bench tops can be made on site for mortaring to concrete, stone or brick supports. Make the formwork out of timber, lined with any suitable thick plastic such as building membrane or old fertiliser sacks. Mix up sufficient concrete of about 4 ballast:1 cement, and spread it evenly into the formwork. Set in some weldmesh or similar to add strength, and leave for at least three days before lifting onto the supports. The top can be as simple or as creative

as you like. Concrete pigments can be used, or mouldings made along the edges or items set into the concrete, as long as they do not interfere with its function as a bench.

BENCHES

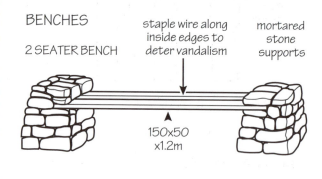

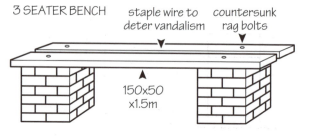

CAST CONCRETE BENCH TOP

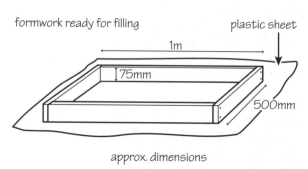

RUSTIC WOODEN BENCH

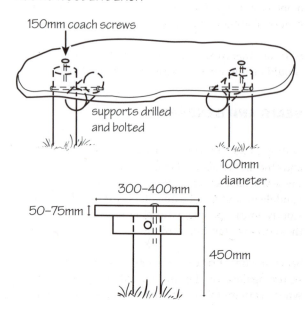

Large logs from fallen or felled trees make good benches. Preferably use ones that have to be moved from roadsides, gardens or other non-wooded sites. Fallen trees in woodland are a potential valuable dead-wood habitat for invertebrates and other organisms, and particularly if scarce in any particular woodland, should be left where they fall. Log seats can be embellished in various ways (p15).

Rustic benches are suitable for locations where they are unlikely to be vandalised.

Small diameter roundwood timber can be used in various ways to make temporary seats. They are unlikely to last more than a season, and possibly only an afternoon, but are fun for children to build. Imaginative bowers, shelters and other structures can be made out of woven willow.

RESTS

Rests or 'perches' should be about 750mm high, securely attached to stout uprights, set firmly into the ground. The top should be narrow and angled, for a person to rest against, but without actually sitting down.

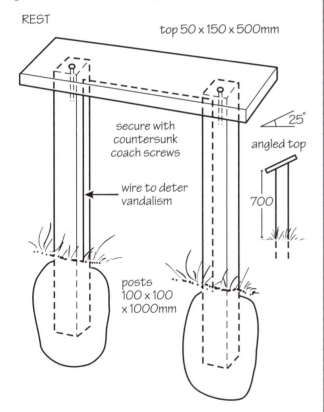

REST

top 50 x 150 x 500mm

secure with countersunk coach screws

wire to deter vandalism

25°

angled top

700

posts 100 x 100 x 1000mm

Signs and information boards

Giving a name and an identity to a site at an early stage helps to generate interest and support. It may also help change perceptions that an area is for example, a wildlife area, and not merely 'neglected'. However, in some locations signs may not be appropriate as they may raise

fears amongst local users that the site and their use of it is going to be greatly altered, even if the actual changes are going to be small. Effective consultation should avert this problem. In some situations, residents may prefer to keep their local sites unsigned, in order to avoid publicising them to people from outside their neighbourhood. It may also be better not to draw attention to new tree planting or ponds, until they are established, or to other features which need protection.

Signs and information boards on sites owned or managed by statutory agencies, local authorities or wildlife trusts may need to follow designs, sizes and methods of production that have been adopted by those organisations. These signs are usually commercially produced. On other sites, there is the opportunity to be innovative, and particularly to use the provision of signs and information as a project to involve local artists, craftsmen, school and college groups.

Five Oaks

nature area

more signboards can be added as required

stone sign

Greenglades Scented Walk

tyres set in concrete

BROAD STREET Community Gardens

Signs, giving the name of the site, and signs giving directions within the site or basic information need to be eyecatching, robust and easy to read. Lettering chiselled into stone, routered in wood, moulded into concrete or formed out of wrought iron can be used, along with other creative techniques. On some urban sites there may be a desire to create a rural, natural feel to the site, in which case simple lettering on natural wood or stone may be appropriate. Other sites may not be limited by this desire, and bright colours or industrial materials may be chosen. Signs which include items linked to the local industrial heritage are effective. It all depends what you want your sign to convey about the site – countryside, industrial heritage, people, community, art or any other value.

Information or interpretation boards give details about the site, usually including a map highlighting various features and facilities, with notes on natural and local history. Again, there is no particular need for urban sites to follow the commercial techniques used for production of boards on rural recreation sites. These boards are expensive to produce and necessarily contain information which cannot be changed. They are useful for tourist sites where most visitors will be on first-time visits. On urban sites, used more often by locals on regular visits, or school groups, the need for permanent interpretive information on site may not be so great. Encouraging people to get to know the site through open days, guided walks and other events may be a better approach, which can involve members of the local community as providers of information, not only recipients. Research and production of information is ideal project work for schools, some of whom have the technology to produce leaflets, tapes and videos, as well as screen-printing and other artwork techniques. This is learning by doing, and site interpretation by and for the community rather than by professionals for the visitor.

TEMPORARY INFORMATION BOARDS

Once the group or project is established enough to have a name, put at least one temporary blackboard or similar at the work site while you are there, so that passers-by can find out who you are and what you are doing.

Chalkboards, permanently fixed on site, are also useful for noting seasonal wildlife to be seen, or for featuring different aspects of the site through the year. They need to be fixed in a prominent location, shielded from the rain. Although the message may not last long, or unwanted ones may appear, such boards linked with frequent wardening and work on the site by staff or local residents may be of more value than permanent information boards.

Temporary signs for supervised nature trails or special events can be neatly and effectively done using labelling systems designed for garden centres. Particularly useful are the plastic or aluminium marker posts with stick-on waterproof labels (bed labels). For supplier see page 52

SEMI-PERMANENT INFORMATION BOARDS

Information boards are frequently a target for vandalism, so beware of spending time and money on something which may only last a short time. Cheap, A4 posters which can easily be replaced are one method. These also allow information to be updated as the project progresses, or to include seasonal information about wildlife to be seen on the site. A4 posters can be laminated in plastic by local printers. 'Correx' plastic corrugated board is a useful material for short-term outdoor signs, as it is lightweight, fairly rigid, and can be written on with waterproof felt markers. It's available from signwriting suppliers. It's also used for packaging so you may be able to find a free source.

An alternative is to build a robust stand, onto which an information board can be fitted when the site is supervised.

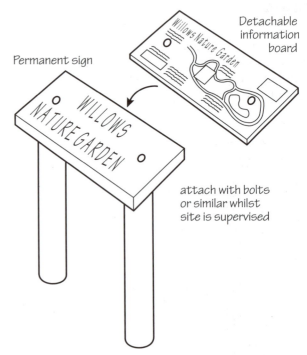

Permanent sign

Detachable information board

WILLOWS NATURE GARDEN

Willows Nature Garden

attach with bolts or similar whilst site is supervised

Consultation about the project with local residents (p27) will have enlisted some local support, and signs should be less prone to vandalism where they are publicising a project in which the local community is involved. Any information boards should be presented in a style and language which is appropriate to the area. Signboards produced by local children are likely to be eye catching and less of a target for vandals than professionally produced boards. For a really expert job harness the skills of local graffiti artists. Feelings of 'local ownership' (p28) should be greatly increased amongst any group who have helped make a sign or information board.

PERMANENT INFORMATION BOARDS

There are numerous commercial processes for producing permanent information boards which may include illustrations and text. Local Yellow Pages list firms under

'Sign makers', and two firms (p131) specialise in producing these for outdoor recreation sites.

GATEWAYS AND ENTRANCES

Gateways and entrances are important to help give an identity to a site, and can incorporate design features to exclude cars or motor-bikes. Support from local arts trusts or businesses may produce sponsorship to commission work by local craftsmen. Wrought-iron, stonework and sculptures in wood have all been used to make imaginative and individual gateways and entrances.

Wrought iron gateway

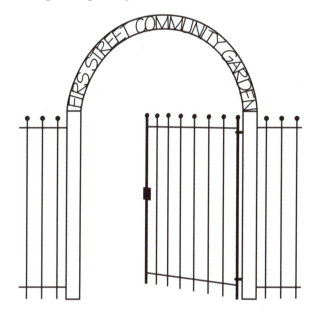

The access controls detailed on page 54 have been developed by Sustrans, for paths designed for use by walkers, cyclists and wheelchair users, but to exclude motorbikes and vehicles. The U shaped passage gives access for wheelchairs and buggies, but is too short for motorbikes to negotiate. The York chicane can be ridden through by a cyclist without dismounting, but can give access for scrambling or dirt motorbikes with high ground clearance. On areas which may attract dirt bikes, the full chicane must be used to exclude them, but these are less convenient for cyclists, who have to dismount. Sustrans recommend steel construction, which is durable and easy to install, and fits in well in most surroundings. The chicanes can be made by local metalworkers. Large boulders can also be used instead of the fence to either side of the chicane. Timber structures can also be used.

Kissing gates are a traditional form of access control, giving access to pedestrians but not to stock. More relevant for today's urban use is a gate which permits access to pedestrians, pushchairs and wheelchairs, but excludes motor-bikes. It may also be useful to discourage bicycle use, although determined cyclists can lift their bikes over most barriers. Steel structures are recommended for many

situations, as they are more difficult to vandalise than wood. Steel allows the use of a curved guard rail, which is a more effective shape for regulating access than the angular shapes to which you are limited by wood. The design shown below is supplied as a single unit, so it is easy and quick to install in a concrete foundation, and difficult to remove. See page 131 for supplier.

WOODSTOCK KISSING GATE FOR
MANUAL WHEELCHAIR ACCESS

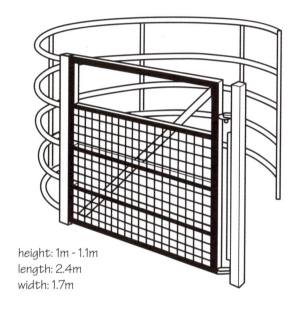

height: 1m - 1.1m
length: 2.4m
width: 1.7m

For further information on gates and stiles, see *Footpaths*, BTCV (1996).

Hedges

Hedges, walls or fences may be needed for security, marking ownership of the site, or dividing areas within it. Ditches or barriers against vehicles may also be needed at the perimeter of the site. Hedges, walls, fences and ditches can all add habitat diversity to a site, without affecting its overall natural development. Creating and maintaining boundary features are suitable projects for groups of volunteers, and can include skills training.

Hedges, walls and fences have the disadvantage that anti-social behaviour can be hidden behind them, out of view from nearby housing and roads. The use and enjoyment of the site may be increased by opening it up and increasing views through it, and from the outside in.

The traditional method of managing hedges in farmland evolved as a method of producing stock-proof barriers from native species of tree. Tree species were selected which produced thick or thorny growth when trimmed or lightly browsed by stock, and which if left to grow, could be partially cut through and laid horizontally to form a barrier, and would then resprout from the base. Some

STANDARD ACCESS CONTROL DETAILS

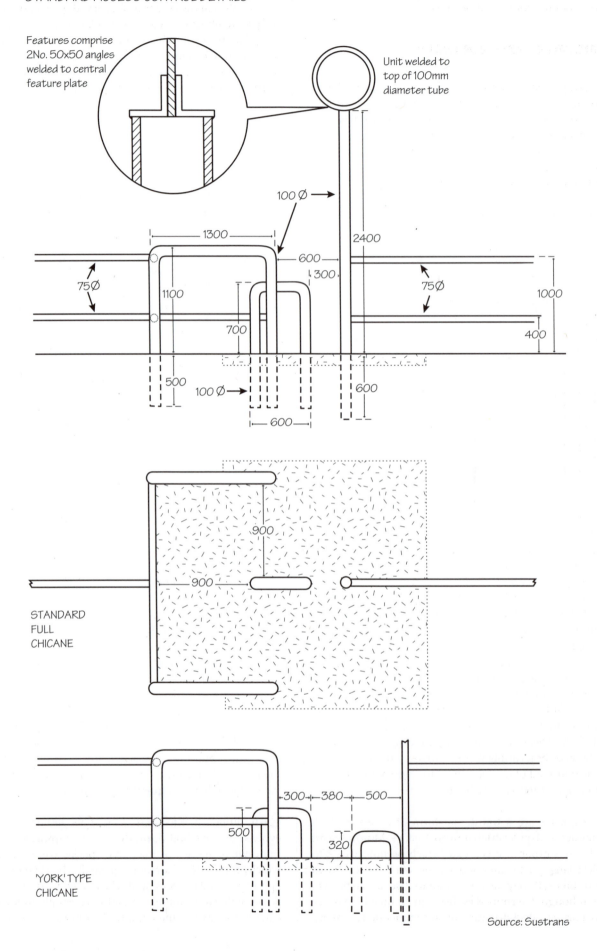

Features comprise 2No. 50x50 angles welded to central feature plate

Unit welded to top of 100mm diameter tube

100 Ø

1300

600

300

2400

75Ø

1100

75Ø

1000

700

400

500

100 Ø

600

600

STANDARD
FULL
CHICANE

900

900

'YORK' TYPE
CHICANE

300 — 380 — 500

500

320

Source: Sustrans

54

hedges were also managed by coppicing or pollarding. As well as stock control and shelter, hedges provided fruit, nuts, fuel and poles for various purposes.

Hedges of hawthorn, blackthorn, beech, hornbeam and other species can be maintained for many years by regular trimming, and if kept to a rounded or 'topped A' shape can remain stockproof. A height of 1.2-1.8m is needed for safe nesting sites for birds. Trimmed hedges come into leaf earlier in the season than the same species in woodland. The common hedging species of hawthorn and blackthorn are anyway early-leafing species, so hedges provide a valuable early season food source for invertebrates, and their predators. The bottoms of dense trimmed hedges are an invaluable habitat for invertebrates, small mammals, reptiles and other creatures, providing a reserve of untrampled, undisturbed habitat, with rotting leaves, dead wood, and crevices in roots and banks.

See Hedge Types diagram on page 56.

Hedges and other boundaries in urban areas rarely need to be stockproof, but being a deterrent to dogs and people may be a useful quality. Planting a hedge with the aim of letting it grow into an informal hedge for future laying may not be appropriate, especially on small, isolated sites. There may not physically be room for the hedge to grow sufficiently tall, and during this phase the dense undisturbed habitat at the bottom may be lost. The physical changes through the life of a laid hedge may also be rather drastic for wildlife, where there is not sufficient length to maintain a rotation of hedge habitats.

Hedges on small urban sites, whether of native or introduced species are best managed as linear thickets or garden hedges. Informal hedges can be planted, of species which tend to grow naturally as multi-stemmed shrubs, but depending on management and use, may not develop the thicket-like growth and undisturbed base of a trimmed or laid hedge. On larger sites, hedges can be grown and laid in the traditional way, or managed by coppicing or pollarding.

Native species for trimmed hedges

Hawthorn, beech, hornbeam, field maple, elm and holly all respond well to trimming and make dense growth. They can be grown singly or mixed in a hedge. Holly is best trimmed annually, but other species can be left for 2 or 3 years, and then cut hard back as necessary. Beech and hornbeam, although deciduous, retain their leaves through the winter. Guelder rose, dog rose, wild privet and gorse can also be mixed in. Blackthorn makes a spiny stockproof and vandalproof hedge if trimmed frequently, but produces suckers which may be a problem. Bramble, ivy and clematis are likely to appear, or can be transplanted if desired. They may need keeping in check to prevent them suppressing other species.

Native species for laying

Species which have plenty of bushy growth that holds in place when laid are preferred, together with thorns to deter stock and people. Stems that are supple and easy to cut are also a useful quality. Hawthorn is easily the best, having these qualities, plus being very hardy and tolerant of different soils, quick growing and easy to propagate. It is the main constituent of most hedge planting schemes. Blackthorn is bushy and thorny, cuts and lays easily, but tends to sucker into adjoining land which may be a disadvantage.

Smoothwood species such as ash, beech, oak, elm, hornbeam, field maple, hazel, willow, sweet chestnut and alder can be laid, but produce rather open growth. These species can also either be coppiced at ground level, or pollarded at hedge-top level.

Native shrubs for informal hedges

Holly, crab apple, box, dogwood, elder, wild privet, spindle, guelder rose and wayfaring tree are suitable for informal hedges or narrow copses. If they are to develop into a useful habitat, sufficient width must be allowed for the shrubs to grow naturally. At least 3m width will normally be necessary, making a narrow woodland feature rather than a hedge.

Note that where hedges are being grant-aided, the choice and proportion of species in the hedge will have to be agreed with the grant-aiding authority, as will the planting distances, fencing or other protection, mulching and aftercare.

There are many species and varieties of introduced shrubs which can be used for ornamental or fruiting hedges. Any good gardening reference book will give details.

Pioneer tree and shrub species of poor, stony soils, such as the native birch and sallow, and the introduced buddleia and cotoneaster, spread naturally by seed onto urban wasteland sites. By their nature they are mostly open growing and light demanding and do not respond well to close planting, trimming or laying. Other species which spread in by suckering from the edges of the site, from dumped garden rubbish or from abandoned gardens are more likely to be suitable hedging species. It may be possible to incorporate existing clumps into new hedges, or to transplant small clumps or self-seeded plants to make an informal hedge of the characteristic local urban species. They will also provide a free source of plants. Cotoneaster, buddleia, berberis and laurel are possible candidates from the naturalised urban flora.

Obtaining hedge plants.

Hawthorn and other species for hedging are widely available from nurseries, and can be obtained by mail

HEDGE TYPES

FACE VIEW

SIDE VIEW

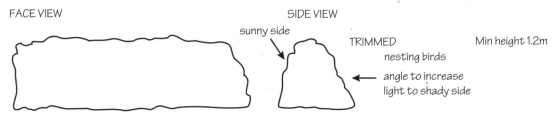

sunny side

TRIMMED   Min height 1.2m

nesting birds

← angle to increase
light to shady side

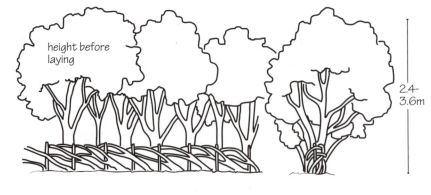

height before
laying

2.4-
3.6m

LAID HEDGE
Lay about every 15 years.
Thorny species, mainly
hawthorn, some blackthorn.
Needs fence to be stock-
proof after laying, and if
it becomes gappy

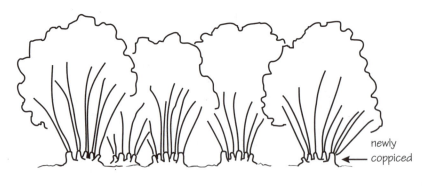

newly
← coppiced

COPPICED HEDGE
Coppice every 10-15 years.
Produces useful poles.
Hazel, sweet chestnut,
willow, ash beech, oak.
Not stockproof

POLLARDED HEDGE
Pollard every 5-10 years.
Old trunks provide useful
habitat. Willow, beech, oak,
sweet chestnut, field maple.
Not stockproof

← 3m →

INFORMAL HEDGE
Many species of shrubs and
small trees suitable.
Allow sufficient width.
Not stockproof

order for planting during the winter. BTCV Enterprises, Conservation Volunteers Northern Ireland and BTCV in Leeds supply hedging plants. Hedging shrubs include hawthorn, blackthorn, guelder rose, wild cherry, hazel, wild privet, field maple, elder and crab apple. The hedge can be left to grow for laying, trimmed regularly, or grown as an informal hedge.

Some individuals and interest groups are keen on retaining local genotypes of plant species (p121). Planting hedges grown from local seed, or propagated vegetatively, is a way of doing this. Individual plants within hedges that are going to be trimmed or laid have potentially a very long life, possibly longer than individuals in woodlands. The seeds or cuttings need to be gathered from an existing hedge, woodland or individual tree that is itself of semi-natural origin. The hawthorn hedges planted during the enclosure movement of the 1800s were from nursery-grown stock, although earlier enclosure hedges may have been grown from locally gathered seed. The best sources are likely to be from long-existing commons or semi-natural woodlands, the relict patches of copse left isolated by development, native species growing in churchyards or hedges of known ancient origin.

Abandoned fertile land such as allotments or farmland may become colonised with species such as hawthorn, blackthorn, ash and oak, rather than the typical pioneer species of poor soils. Where permission can be obtained, these could provide a source of native hedging plants, which although of unknown provenance, will at least be known to be successfully adapted to local conditions. Transplant seedlings or small plants in winter.

Planning and planting a new hedge

Choose the species which are appropriate to the type of hedge you want to create (see above), and which suit the soil and locality. Any existing vegetation on the site, and nearby woods or hedges will be a guide.

To be a useful habitat and a barrier, most hedging plants need planting in a double staggered row. The distance depends on how dense the growth needs to be, and whether the hedge is to be trimmed or laid. Trimmed hedges generally need to have plants closer spaced than hedges for laying. Spacing varies between 200-300mm in the row, with rows 150-400mm apart. Where space or funds are limited, plant in a single row, 200-300mm apart.

Planting can be 'on the flat', or with a ditch to one side, or on a bank with or without a ditch. Where there is the space and time available, the creation of a bank and ditch will provide a range of microhabitats, as well as creating an interesting landscape feature. The ditch may be useful for protecting the young plants, or it may invite children to jump and slide and possibly destroy the hedge. Warm, sheltered south facing hedge banks are particularly valuable habitats. Where the water table is high, the creation of a well-drained bank will assist the growth of hedge plants, and the water-filled ditch will be an additional useful habitat, so long as it does not drain and spoil any adjoining wetland.

Ground preparation on fertile soils such as abandoned allotments, parks or gardens involves removing the existing grass sward or other vegetation. This can be done by ploughing, using a rotavator or hand digging, or by spraying a contact or translocated herbicide. Hedging plants, normally transplants 30-45cm high, are then notch planted and well trodden in (chapter 6). Planting is best done in November, but can be done any time while the plants are not in leaf, from late October to March.

Establishing a hedge on urban sites with little or no soil, or with limitations of toxicity, pH and other factors is not so easy. Digging a trench and filling it with imported topsoil is a possibility, but may be expensive and not necessarily successful. In poorly drained compacted substrates the planting trench is likely to become waterlogged in winter and dry in summer. On well drained substrates it will support a strong growth of grasses and other herbs which will compete with the hedge plants. On these sites, the growing of a traditional dense stockproof hedge may not be a sensible or achievable aim, whereas an informal hedge of native and introduced species typical of the site or similar sites nearby is more appropriate.

New hedges may be vulnerable to trampling, people taking short cuts, and vandalism. Stock netting or chestnut paling can be used (p61), though this may itself be vandalised or stolen. Protective netting against stock should be at least 1m from the hedge. On larger sites, new hedge plants may need protecting against rabbits, preferably by using rabbit netting. Individual spiral guards can be used, but the aim is normally to prune plants for short, bushy growth, to which a spiral guard cannot be fitted. Various shrub shelters and other products are available, but add considerably to the cost of the hedge. Keeping the base of the hedge weed free removes cover for voles, which may otherwise gnaw the bark. This can be done by hand weeding, herbicides or mulching roll. However, mulching roll or mats may themselves provide cover for voles.

Ancient and new planting methods

Hedges in urban areas do not usually need to be stockproof, nor need to follow the specifications of grant-aiding authorities or the traditions of rural hedging. There is room for non-standard techniques of planting and training, as well as choice of species.

A planting technique used by the Romans was to place seeds of suitable species into the fibres of a rope, and then lay the rope along a prepared furrow to form the hedgeline. Similar methods are recorded of twisting straw into loose ropes and setting the seed within it. The likely success is not known, but it could be fun to try where the outcome is not too critical.

Layering is an ancient technique for propagating plants. This involves pegging down a live stem from a plant, which then produces roots and new plants at points along the stem. This technique is sometimes used when restoring an old gappy hedge, to produce new plants to fill the gaps. A similar technique can be used with new plants, by laying them horizontally instead of planting them upright, giving more plants for your money. Hawthorn, blackthorn, holly, crab apple, cherry and rose can be successfully layered. Climbers such as clematis and honeysuckle can be propagated this way to grow through hedges and fences. Tall, leggy plants which may otherwise be rejected are good material for horizontal planting. You may be able to get some publicity out of a horizontal planting project, but make sure you present yourself as someone who knows what they're doing!

HORIZONTAL PLANTING

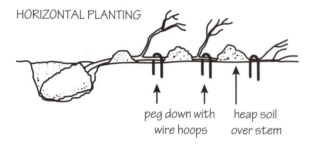

peg down with wire hoops

heap soil over stem

Another old method, made easier by modern machinery, is to transplant mature hedge plants. Hedge moving is now sometimes specified in road widening schemes, as it is possible to dig up mature, trimmed hedges in winter, and transplant them to another location. Many gardeners have successfully moved large garden shrubs, often with little regard to season. Old hedgerows should not be dug up, but any that cannot be saved in situ can at least be transplanted. Keep an eye on local development work which may be a source of reject hedge or garden shrubs. Evergreens should be left unpruned, but others can be pruned back at almost any season to lessen transpiration, reduce the bulk for easy moving, and to make them look unattractive to potential thieves. Mature shrubs, securely planted, should be robust enough to survive casual vandalism.

Care of the young hedge

The care is similar to that of young trees (p66), and involves mulching and weeding for the first three or so years. Watering through a drought in the first season after planting may be necessary.

Hawthorn and blackthorn are normally cut back hard to 100mm above the ground immediately after planting in autumn, or if planted in early spring, cut back in the following autumn. This encourages bushy growth. The hedge is then pruned back by a third in late winter for the following 3-4 years. Pruning immediately after planting also has the advantage of making the new plants less visible, and less easy to break or pull out. Where vandal deterrence is important, all the species mentioned above, except holly, can be hard pruned after planting.

An alternative to early pruning is to lay the hedge in the year after planting. The young stem is cut half to three-quarters through at 100mm above ground level, bent over and the twiggy growth is anchored into its neighbour. The shrub regrows from the cut, and from along the bent stem, making a thick, bushy hedge. This has been successfully done with hawthorn, and may work with other species. At worst, if the stem breaks, the plant has merely been pruned.

LAYING NEWLY PLANTED HEDGE

strong shoots arise from laid stem

shoots at cut

Hedge laying

A new hedge is normally laid when it has reached the height of about 2.4-3.6m tall. The main stems are selected for pleachers, which will be partially cut and laid. The first group of pleachers are cut and laid to one side, until there is sufficient room to lay a pleacher into the hedge. The cut in the pleacher should be about 30-100mm above ground, and just over three-quarters through so that the stem bends without being forced. The pleacher should lay upwards at an angle of between 25-45 degrees, and angled across the width of the hedge. Prepared stakes of hazel or ash, or commercial softwood stakes, about 1.4-1.8m long, are then knocked in and the pleachers woven between them. Slender binders of hazel, willow, clematis or other available materials are then twisted along the top to hold the pleachers in place. The brushy ends of the laid pleachers are best left uncut, to protect the hedge from being pulled apart by vandals. Newly laid hedges also unfortunately make interesting adventure play structures

BASIC HEDGE LAYING

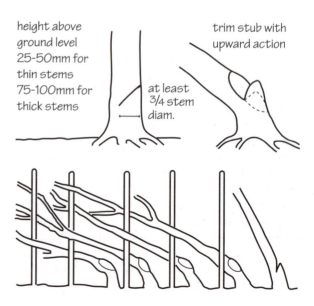

height above ground level 25-50mm for thin stems 75-100mm for thick stems

at least 3/4 stem diam.

trim stub with upward action

for children to climb and jump on. A few strands of barbed wire should act as a deterrent during the first winter after laying. Remove the following spring.

For further information on hedge laying, including restoring old hedges, see *Hedging*, BTCV (2002).

Walls

Walls can be used to define the boundaries or different areas within the site. Retaining walls can be built to make changes of level within the site. Dry stone walls provide a valuable habitat for invertebrates, amphibians, reptiles and small mammals which shelter or hibernate in the crevices. Walls also create conditions of shelter and warmth, shade and damp, providing microhabitats for various organisms.

Walls can be built out of any suitable material on the site, including stone, brick and building rubble, or a combination of materials. Concrete rubble from hard standings can be broken up into pieces for use like stone, and weather to a reasonable appearance after a year or two.

Coping stones on dry stone walls are normally mortared in position, to prevent them being dislodged or removed. On sites where vandalism or theft is possible, the wall itself may have to be mortared. To retain some habitat value, leave some crevices unmortared, leading into the centre of the wall.

The dimensions of a free standing dry stone wall will depend on the available stone, and the purpose of the wall. A bottom width of about 600mm should be sufficient for a wall 1m high, increasing to a width of 900mm for a wall 1.3m high. Start by marking out the base of the wall, and digging out a footing deep enough to take the largest stones, which will form the foundation. Stones or rubble are then built up in layers, the largest at the bottom, trying to fit each stone so that it is solid and crosses a gap. The middle of the wall is carefully packed with small stones as work progresses. Occasional large stones or 'throughs' can be placed across to tie the outer faces together.

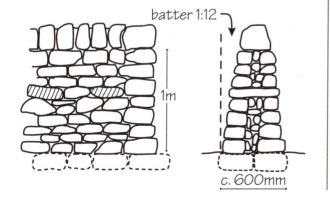

Retaining walls are built in a similar way, backfilling as work progresses. High retaining walls holding back a large amount of backfill may be a hazard to safety, so a maximum of about 600mm height is probably suitable, especially where the walling material is variable or vandalism likely.

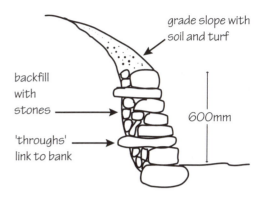

For further information see *Dry Stone Walling*, BTCV (1999). Mortared walls, built of stone, brick, block or a variety of materials, may be preferable to dry stone walls to discourage vandalism or for safety reasons. The construction of garden walls is well described in the many books available on garden construction, for example *The Small Garden*, Brooks, John (1977).

Effective retaining walls can be built out of old tyres, stacked either to make a near vertical wall, or as a sloping bank. The latter makes an irresistible play feature for children, and planting in the pockets is almost certainly doomed. Painting the tyres is a more reliable method of brightening them.

Wall building is best done near paths, site entrances or prominent parts of the site, where they will either have a function to mark a boundary, improve the site appearance or to direct users, and where the walls are overlooked to deter vandalism. Using piles of existing stone or rubble to build walls with no particular purpose other than habitat improvement may be self-defeating, as the pile of stone is likely to be a more valuable habitat than a wall, and is also less likely to be vandalised.

Mortared walls in community gardens and other supervised sites can incorporate handmade tiles, mosaics, sculptures and so on, and their building can be linked with local arts projects. Crevices or specially-made bricks (see page 131 for supplier) can be incorporated for animal homes.

As historical features containing interesting geological examples, walls in urban areas have great potential for study and interpretation. The Geologists Association has promoted 'The Wall Game', to encourage the use of walls for education. New walls can also be built out of a variety of local stones and reclaimed building material. This may be a good way of preserving fragments from derelict buildings which have to be demolished for safety or other reasons, thus keeping a link with the past.

Native or introduced climbing plants can be grown up walls in almost any situation, to provide the benefits of greenery and flowers for people and wildlife. Of the native plants, ivy is self-clinging and common everywhere, and is of great value for invertebrates, birds and other animals. Consult a gardening reference book, for example *Gardening on Walls*, Grey-Wilson, Christopher and Matthews, Victoria (1983) for information on introduced climbing plants.

Fences and barriers

Fences for managing semi-natural green spaces in urban areas may be needed for the following:

- to protect new plantings of trees, shrubs and hedges.

- to prevent young children having unsupervised access to ponds and other water features

- to secure community gardens, play centre gardens and other small sites against improper use. Many of these sites are attached to buildings or are supervised during the day.

- to prevent vehicle access to a site

All fences may attract vandalism or theft, or may by their presence draw attention to the feature you are intending to protect. Some may be vandalised by people who feel a perceived right of access is being infringed, or because the fence represents authority or interference. Local consultation can reduce this. Note should always be taken of existing desire lines, and fencing fitted in to retain these if possible. Some areas have abandoned the use of any timber fencing, because of theft and vandalism. Stock netting is easy to vandalise with wire cutters, or may be stolen for re-use. Anything reasonably substantial made of metal may be stolen for its scrap value.

Protection for tree planting

The standard advice for tree planting is to fence against the trampling of people, and against the trampling and browsing of stock. Rabbits, voles and other animals may be also be a problem (ch 6). However, for small patches of tree planting on urban sites this advice may not apply, and the advice from several different urban areas is not to bother. The fencing itself may be vandalised or stolen, and it will attract attention to the trees. Vandals can easily climb in and destroy the trees if they so wish, and the fenced areas become a focus for litter and dumping. In Tipton, West Midlands, where there is a strong tradition of keeping horses and ponies within the urban area, the vegetation within fenced tree planting areas is seen as free grazing, and owners cut the fences and put up temporary barriers to corral their horses within the fenced 'exclosures'. In some areas chestnut paling has been successfully used around tree planting areas, as this is difficult to climb and rather time-consuming to take apart.

Limited trampling by people and dogs within new tree plantings can help keep down competing vegetation.

Small tree planting areas within school grounds or parks where there is some level of supervision may be worth fencing, to protect against heavy trampling by children playing ball games and so on. A stock netting fence of the type shown below would be suitable.

There may be a problem where grant-aiding authorities require fencing or individual tree protection for tree-planting schemes, which are usually more costly than the trees they are meant to protect, and which may be counter-productive.

Full details of fencing against various types of stock and wild animals is given in *Fencing* (BTCV, 1985).

Safety fencing

This may be needed around ponds and water features or along roadsides, particularly on sites used by young children and schools. For school sites, consult with the local education authority. Strained stock netting, post and rail with or without netting, chestnut paling or board fences may be suitable. These are not all proof against a child determined to get over, but should act as a warning and a reminder. On sites with particular hazards such as old mine workings, much higher security fencing will be needed, which should be erected by a specialist firm.

Thick growth of bramble alongside any of the above type of fence makes an effective barrier for safety and security.

Security fencing

Most community gardens are made in existing gardens with walls, hedges or fences that give some measure of security. Allotments or permaculture gardens are vulnerable to thieving of vegetables and produce, and ornamental gardens may have newly planted shrubs dug up, turves removed or other materials stolen. The more intensively the garden is planted and landscaped, the more vulnerable it is. Security fencing 1.8m or higher may be the only answer, but is expensive and not usually covered by grant-aid. A community garden with high security fencing is something of a contradiction in terms. Supervision, frequent use and involvement by the local community will help protect a site, but it may be that investment of time and money on a site where these factors are not present is bound for disappointment. A less ambitious project, and a slow build up of local involvement may be the better approach.

STOCK NETTING – lightweight

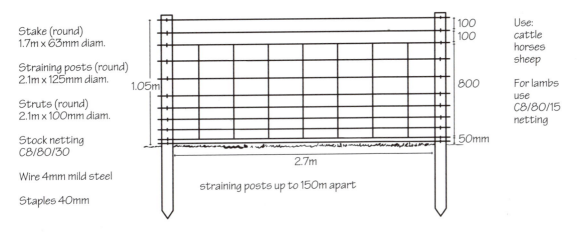

Stake (round)
1.7m x 63mm diam.

Straining posts (round)
2.1m x 125mm diam.

Struts (round)
2.1m x 100mm diam.

Stock netting
C8/80/30

Wire 4mm mild steel

Staples 40mm

1.05m

100
100

800

50mm

2.7m

straining posts up to 150m apart

Use:
cattle
horses
sheep

For lambs
use
C8/80/15
netting

NAILED POST AND RAIL – preserved softwood

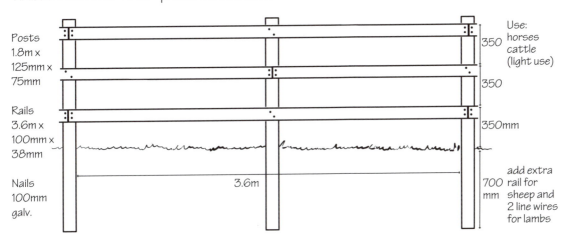

Posts
1.8m x
125mm x
75mm

Rails
3.6m x
100mm x
38mm

Nails
100mm
galv.

3.6m

350

350

350mm

700
mm

Use:
horses
cattle
(light use)

add extra
rail for
sheep and
2 line wires
for lambs

CHESTNUT PALING

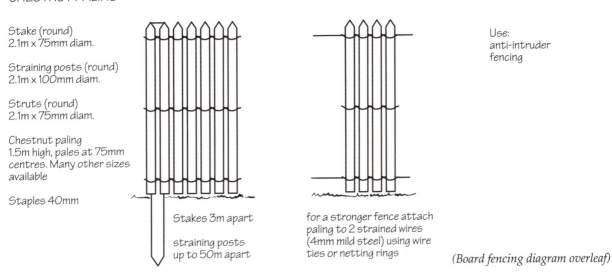

Stake (round)
2.1m x 75mm diam.

Straining posts (round)
2.1m x 100mm diam.

Struts (round)
2.1m x 75mm diam.

Chestnut paling
1.5m high, pales at 75mm
centres. Many other sizes
available

Staples 40mm

Stakes 3m apart

straining posts
up to 50m apart

for a stronger fence attach
paling to 2 strained wires
(4mm mild steel) using wire
ties or netting rings

Use:
anti-intruder
fencing

(Board fencing diagram overleaf)

Barriers

Barriers may be neccessary to stop people driving vehicles and motor bikes onto a site. Low 'trip fencing' of round timbers on low posts, wired to deter vandals with saws, may be sufficient.

In other areas, large blocks of stone positioned by digger have been found to be the only effective method. Another technique is to use a digger to dig a wide ditch, about a metre deep, with a steep face on the side away from the road. Depending on the location and whether or not it holds water, it may need marking with posts or fencing for safety reasons.

Wide shallow ditches or small ponds are also effective as long as they stay water-filled. Motor-cycle access to part of the woods managed by *Woodscape* (p80) was prevented by damming a stream to make a small pond across the access point. Access on foot was retained by placing large stepping stones across the pond, making an attractive feature as well as an effective barrier.

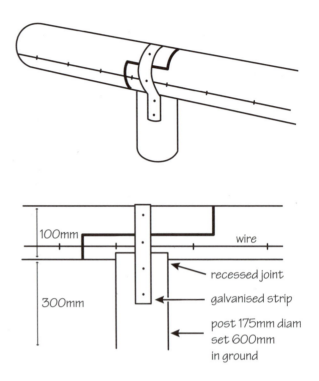

100mm

300mm

wire

recessed joint

galvanised strip

post 175mm diam
set 600mm
in ground

BOARD FENCING – preserved softwood

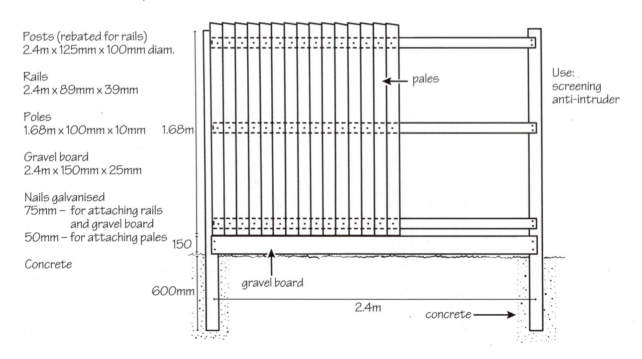

Posts (rebated for rails)
2.4m x 125mm x 100mm diam.

Rails
2.4m x 89mm x 39mm

Poles
1.68m x 100mm x 10mm   1.68m

Gravel board
2.4m x 150mm x 25mm

Nails galvanised
75mm – for attaching rails
         and gravel board
50mm – for attaching pales   150

Concrete

pales

Use:
screening
anti-intruder

600mm

gravel board

2.4m

concrete

6   Trees and woodlands

Trees in urban areas

Trees in urban areas bestow many benefits. They give shelter from the wind and shade from the summer sun. They filter noise and dust, and help remove pollutants from the air. They also give privacy and seclusion, soothing greenery and a natural texture to offset the artificial surfaces of roads and buildings. They provide a home for wildlife, and, through old coppices, pollards, and mature native trees, a direct link with the past. Trees are a natural play feature for children, for climbing and swinging, and providing sticks, nuts and leaves for play. Trees make us all feel better. Patients in hospital rooms with a green view recover more quickly than those looking onto buildings, possibly because such views are soothing and invoke feelings of hope.

Trees in cities and towns are generally associated with the affluent areas, which had the luxury of space and alternative fuel supplies so that existing mature trees could be retained, and new trees planted. Green views can thus invoke feelings of security and affluence, shown by the fact that mature trees enhance property values. Developers of new 'executive' homes pay premiums for existing wooded sites.

Trees in urban areas also have disadvantages. Trees too close to buildings can block sunlight and views. Summer transpiration can dry out clay soils causing subsidence and damage to pavements, pipes and walls. Honeydew from aphids and autumn leaf fall can be seen as causing a nuisance. High hedges, copses and dense woodland growth can create a fear that the seclusion they offer will conceal criminal behaviour, both against property or person. Perhaps the fact that these woodland features are accepted in affluent areas is because there is less fear of crime against the person, although property crime may be high. You may feel comfortable walking through a woodland surrounded by houses with burglar alarms, because the fear of personal attack is low. In a similar woodland in a less affluent area, crimes against the person, thus fears of suffering it, are higher.

URBAN WOODLAND DESIGN

To bestow these benefits, while reducing the disadvantages, perceived or actual, attention needs to be given to the following:

- Balance of tree cover with open space: People's fear of woodland can be addressed by careful design of urban woodlands so that there is plenty of open space, with wide rides and avenues and areas of rough and mown grass.

- Management of trees and woodland shrubs: Areas of natural woodland growth, with shrubs and thick cover which is beneficial for wildlife, need balancing with areas of clear-stemmed trees with open ground beneath, where most people will feel more secure. This open type of woodland can be achieved by careful choice of species and by pruning of the lower branches of trees.

- Use of the woodland: Wide, clear paths in attractive surroundings will encourage daily use of woodlands. Special events, frequent management, use by school groups and other activities will ensure that the woodland is inviting to all legitimate users.

- Choice of species: Near buildings, paths and car-parks suitable species need to be chosen which will minimise problems with roots, honeydew and leaf fall. Non-native species may be appropriate for small woodlands, parks and other areas planted for amenity and wildlife purposes.

TREE AND WOODLAND PROJECTS

There are two main types of volunteer work associated with trees in urban areas:

- Establishing new trees: This can vary from individual trees in gardens, through small copses up to areas of many thousands of new trees.

- Managing existing trees, from small copses to large woodlands: Volunteer involvement in managing existing woodlands covers a range of work, from clearance of rubbish, improvement of footpaths or other access work, through to the strictly 'woodland' work of coppicing, tree felling and planting.

Thinning of trees and clearance of undergrowth to 'open up' woodlands is often part of this work, because of the desire for fairly open, user-friendly woods, where people feel safe. Glades, meadows and ponds within woodlands are also valuable. Management of woodlands may therefore include much of the work described in other chapters of this handbook.

This chapter first describes the basic rules for successful tree establishment, which are common to all tree planting, from gardens up to large woodlands. The remainder of the chapter is mainly concerned with the establishment and management of small woods.

Basic rules for tree establishment

These apply to almost all situations, and for any numbers of trees, from small groups to new woodlands.

SIZE OF PLANTING STOCK

Plant small. Young trees for planting are referred to as either tree seedlings, transplants or undercuts, depending on how they've been grown, and are usually 30-60cm high. A 'whip' is any of these, with a single leading stem pruned of side growth, whereas a 'feather' has several side shoots. Young trees have many advantages over larger stock. They establish quickly, and in a few growing seasons, catch up or overtake trees planted as standards. Young trees do not need stakes to hold them firm, and develop a strong anchorage of roots as they grow. Trees planted as standards (1.7-1.8m tall) and then staked tend to produce less vigorous root systems, which are unable to support them when the stakes are removed. Standards need watering during dry spells for at least the first season, whereas smaller plants with a better ratio of roots to shoots can flourish through droughts without watering. Small trees are less prone to vandalism, because they are less noticeable, and less inviting to pull over and break. If they are damaged, the loss is minor as they usually regrow. Seedlings or transplants (see below) are very much cheaper than standards. Where people want to plant standards for 'instant' results, or because they think this is a short-cut to creating a parkland landscape, they must be persuaded otherwise!

Native trees are available from tree nurseries in the sizes given below. Larger sizes may also be available, but are not recommended for the reasons given above. 1 year trees are seedlings that have not been transplanted. Transplanted trees produce a better ratio of roots to shoots than do non-transplanted trees, and establish better when moved to their final planting position. '1 u 1' indicates that a one year old seedling has been undercut with a spade, to stimulate fibrous root growth, and then grown on for another year in the same position. Some nurseries may also supply trees grown in containers. Native evergreens such as holly and juniper do not transplant well as bare root plants. Other plants may be pot-grown to allow planting at any time of year. Pot-grown plants are more expensive than plants supplied bare-root.

Height in cm	
1 year	20-40
Transplant	40-60
Transplant	60-90
Transplant	90-120

SPACING

Trees and shrubs for small copses or woodlands should be planted at close spacings, of about 2m, and then later thinned. Even for intended groups of three or four trees, it is more effective to plant 30-40 whips, and then thin out at about 5 years and again at 10 years to retain the trees you want. Mass planting allows for losses, and creates a sheltered shrubby habitat which mutually benefits the young trees. The whole area can be fenced, or the vegetation allowed to grow up around the plots of trees so they are less likely to be trampled. Vary the spacing to avoid planting in rows (p71), leave plenty of space for rides and glades (p68) and choose mixtures of trees and shrubs which suit the local conditions and the type of woodland you want to create (pp69-70 and 72-77).

Unless the failure rate has been very high, thinning is essential to avoid creating a dense, shaded wood of spindly trees and straggling shrubs with little ground flora.

From the 'thicket stage', at 5-10 years, thinning can be used to develop a range of woodland types. Depending on the species used, these types may vary from a forest of tall trees with a closed canopy, a wood with all the woodland layers, through to individual trees in grassland.

It is important that the local community are informed and consulted about management of the developing wood, to avoid misunderstandings. In particular, the thicket stage can be seen as 'scrubby and overgrown'. Conversely, any thinning may be viewed as destructive. In the short term thinning will cause losses to wildlife, but in the longer term is essential to create an attractive, valuable and useful habitat. Thinnings can be chipped for mulch to be used either within the wood or elsewhere, or used for garden poles, firewood or other uses.

SOIL

Topsoil is not necessary even on sites with stony substrates. Topsoil can be a hindrance because it encourages lush weed growth which competes with the trees. Imported topsoil will bring in unwanted weed species, and make it more difficult to encourage the development of a woodland flora. Even on very altered substrates, it is usually better to work with the existing conditions, and make the most of any natural regeneration of trees and other plants, non-natives included.

It is not necessary when planting whips to dig a planting hole and fill it with topsoil. Planting holes tend to become either waterlogged in poorly drained soils, or dry out in stony soils, and even if tree root growth within the planting hole is good, it may not root into the surrounding subsoil. Fertiliser may be necessary in some situations to help new trees establish, or to accelerate natural regeneration. Fertiliser application must be accompanied by effective

THE BEST WAY TO PLANT

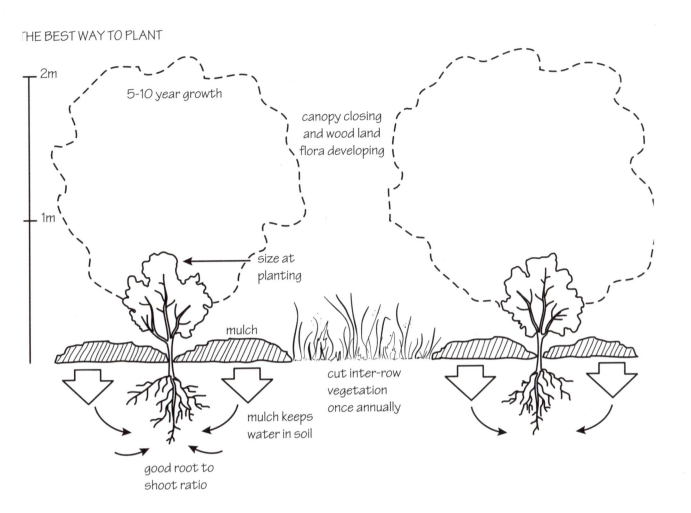

2m

5-10 year growth

canopy closing
and wood land
flora developing

size at
planting

1m

mulch

cut inter-row
vegetation
once annually

mulch keeps
water in soil

good root to
shoot ratio

THE WORST WAY TO PLANT

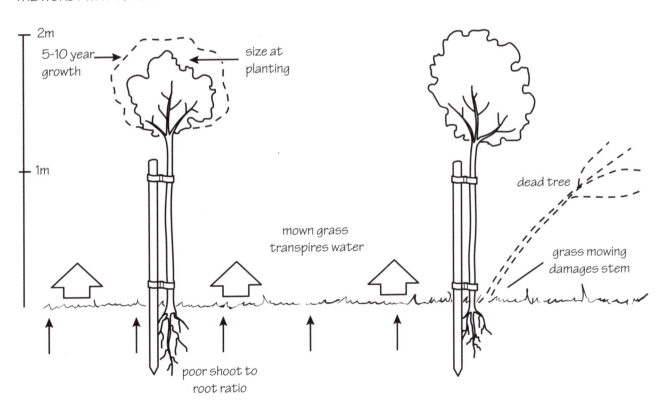

2m

5-10 year
growth

size at
planting

1m

mown grass
transpires water

dead tree

grass mowing
damages stem

poor shoot to
root ratio

weed control, or the fertiliser may be counter-productive by merely encouraging growth of weeds, which are able to take up the fertiliser more quickly than the trees can. Areas of disturbed ground, industrial sites, and those that are supporting little vegetation even after some years will need checking before planting. Soils should be analysed for phosphorus, potassium and magnesium, and soil pits dug 700mm deep to check for drainage and compaction. Badly compacted soils will need ripping to improve drainage. For further information see *Creating and managing Woodlands around Towns*, Forestry Commission (1995).

WEED CONTROL AND CONSERVATION OF SOIL MOISTURE

Weed control for the first three to five years is essential. An area of at least one metre diameter around each tree should be kept free of weeds. This can be done with herbicide, mulches of various types or by hand weeding.

Weeds interfere physically with tree growth, and compete for soil moisture and nutrients. Most soil moisture is lost by transpiration from leaves, with smaller losses from bare soil. If these losses can be reduced, there will be more soil moisture available for the young trees. Nutrients only become available when the soil is damp.

The worst surround to a young tree is mown grass, which effectively sucks the water out of the ground. The best is to start with damp, weed free ground, which is then covered with a mulch. The difference between the two in tree survival and growth is startling.

In general, herbicides are most effective for the 'spot treatment' of a one metre diameter area around a tree. Mulch covering one square metre is less effective, as weeds root in from the sides. If a larger area can be mulched, this becomes more effective than using a herbicide.

Herbicides

The herbicide propyzamide is a pre-emergent herbicide, which can be applied immediately after the trees have been planted, but is only effective on bare soil. It should be applied before the end of January in warmer districts, and before the end of February in the north and east of the UK. Propyzamide in the formulation Kerb Granules is approved for amateur use. When planting into turf, the most effective herbicide is glyphosate, available through garden centres and other retail outlets under various trade names. Glyphosate can be applied by hand spray on unwanted vegetation any time during the growing season. It is most effective when used at the time of maximum growth of the weed plant, but before it flowers. Follow manufacturer's instructions when using herbicides.

No-one under 16 years should apply herbicides. Professional herbicides from agricultural suppliers, or any herbicides used in return for payment to the group or an individual must only be applied by trained and qualified persons.

Mulch

Any material which suppresses weed growth, so retaining soil moisture, can be used as a mulch. Various mulch mats are available from tree planting suppliers, which are ready-cut with a slot for easy fitting around the tree. Alternatively, mats can be made out of thick dark plastic, carpet, underlay, linoleum or any other sheet material. On free draining soils, cover as much of the tree planting area as possible for the best results. A black plastic sheet, for example 10 x 8m and mulching 40 trees at 2m spacing, will result in very fast tree growth. Lack of direct rainfall appears not to be a problem, due to sideways movement of soil water. On damp soils, total coverage may cause waterlogging beneath the mat which is detrimental to the trees. When the material is removed, the weed-free ground beneath is ideal for establishing a woodland flora. Flexible material should be anchored around the edge with pegs, stones or soil. Covering sheet material with stones, gravel or bark will anchor and disguise it, as well as discouraging voles from gaining access to the tree stems from beneath the sheet. Sheet material designed specifically for mulching should not fade or become brittle in sunlight, but other materials probably will, and a covering will protect it. Non-biodegradable sheet materials should be removed after about three years.

Loose material which can be used as a mulch includes wood chippings, coarse compost, composted bark, rotted manure, stones and rubble. A layer at least 75mm deep should be used.

See *Trees and Weeds*, Forestry Commission (1987) for details.

PROTECTION

Young trees may be vulnerable to damage by rabbits, voles, squirrels, deer, grazing stock and vandals. In urban areas it is generally best to use as little protection as possible, to avoid drawing attention to the trees. Fencing, tree shelters and spiral guards all attract attention and vandalism. Where rabbits are a problem, use spiral guards fitted to the trees. Where vole damage occurs, use herbicides rather than sheet mulches for weed control. Voles use the cover of sheet material or tall grasses to reach the tree stems. Only ring-fence the planted areas when it is necessary to keep out horses or other grazing stock. However, it is not unknown for horse-owners then to break through the fences in order to take advantage of the grazing within! Deer damage is unlikely to cause significant losses in most urban areas.

Squirrels can damage or kill established trees by stripping the bark, especially of smooth-barked trees such as beech and sycamore. Trees are most vulnerable when about 16m top height (10-40 years). It may be advisable to avoid planting these species on sites where squirrels are numerous. Cherry, lime and ash are less susceptible to damage.

HOW TO PLANT

The young trees should be supplied from the nursery in special sealed plastic sacks which are white on the outside and black on the inside, to prevent the roots from drying or warming. If the trees can't be planted straight away, they can be stored as they are in a cool dark building for two or three weeks. Handle and store the sacks carefully to avoid bruising the roots. If there is no suitable indoor storage, the trees should be taken out of the sacks and placed in a shallow trench with the roots covered with soil. Transfer of bare-root stock from bag to trench, from bag to bag or during final planting must be done carefully but speedily, so that roots never for a second become dry. Any drying will reduce their chance of successful establishment.

Do not plant when there is a ground frost or in very cold winds. Preferably choose a still, misty, damp day when drying of the roots will be minimised. When you are ready to plant, transfer the trees quickly from the sealed bags to special planting satchels or clean plastic sacks. Do not use unwashed fertiliser sacks as the residue may damage the roots.

To plant, make a notch in the shape of an L, H or T, and lift the turf forward with the spade. Plant the tree by gently pushing it down into the notch, and then withdrawing it slightly to spread the roots. The existing soil mark on the root collar indicates the correct planting depth. Firm the turf down with the foot.

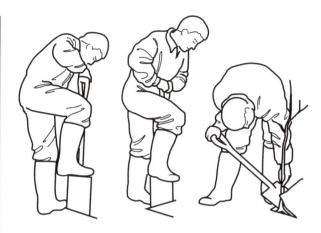

Site check list

As an initial site check, before planning new planting, consider the following points.

The existing vegetation may need surveying to assess its existing ecological value, in order to avoid the danger of spoiling something of value by planting trees on it.

There may be sufficient seed sources nearby so that natural regeneration of trees would proceed fairly rapidly if grazing or mowing ceased. Check for natural regeneration at the edges of the site or in any protected pockets, or look at any similar sites nearby which are not grazed or mown. Natural regeneration of pioneer species such as birch or willow is likely to occur quickly into sparse ground vegetation on stony substrates, abandoned railway tracks, bonfire sites and so on, but will be slower into a thick grass sward.

Check the site for underground and overhead services, and for the proximity of buildings. The main problem with trees

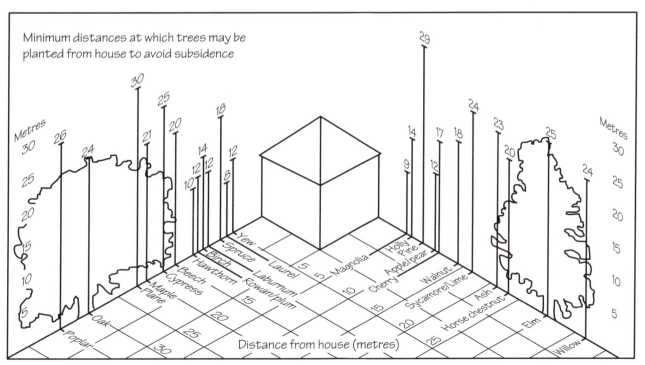

Source: The Subsidence Claims Advisory Bureau

close to buildings occurs on clay soils, which may shrink during a dry summer as trees remove water from the ground by transpiration. When this is not replaced by rainfall, the clay shrinks, causing subsidence and cracking of buildings and pavements. Broadleaved trees remove more water than evergreens and conifers. The table on page 67 shows the minimum distances from buildings at which trees can be planted to avoid the danger of subsidence. Note that these are 'safe' minimum distances, as recommended by house insurers. Many existing urban trees are far nearer to buildings than this recommendation. With drought an increasing problem, it is suggested that these guidelines are followed for new planting in clay soils. For advice on whether a particular location is subject to subsidence, consult with local householders, or inquire at estate agents or local builders who will be aware of any problem areas.

When mature, will the trees block views, or shade buildings or gardens? Check carefully on an accurate plan, and on site, and consult with local residents. Photos with mature trees 'superimposed' will give a good idea of what the mature planting will look like. Computer software packages are available for garden and landscape design, which can produce sophisticated graphics and 3D.

Has the fear of woodland harbouring crime been effectively addressed? Frequent wardening and the use of the woodland by the community for various activities will create feelings of safety. Careful design of paths and glades, with plenty of open, light woodland helps people feel safe. It will also attract more people to use it, making it safer.

Woodland specification

Most tree planting projects will require the drawing up of plans and specifications. The following information may be needed.

Background to project

This should include details of how the initial idea came about, who has been consulted to date, and responsibilities for the management of the project.

Site description

A description of the physical characteristics of the site should be made, including size, slope, drainage, soil, existing vegetation, underground services and any other relevant details. A site plan is needed to a suitable scale, usually 1:200 for small sites, and 1:500 for sites of about one hectare and over. The same plan can be used for designing the planting layout and access routes.

Objectives for the site

These may include use by the public, involvement of volunteers in practical management, habitat creation and timber production.

Woodland type

Types of woodland include coppice, coppice with standards, high forest and parkland wood. The choice will depend on the physical characteristics of the site, the objectives of the woodland, and resources available for future management. The choice of species and planting mixture is closely linked to the woodland type. On larger sites, different areas or plots can be planted and managed in different ways. For each plot, list the woodland type and species. For further details on woodland type see pages 69-70 and for species, see pages 72-77.

Planting details

This includes the spacing between trees (p64), pattern of species mix (p71), protection (p66) and weed control (p66).

Paths and access

Plan main access routes and techniques of any path construction needed. Show areas where access is to be encouraged or discouraged and how this is to be achieved. For further details on access see chapter 5.

Open space management

Glades and open spaces within the site will need management by mowing or grazing. More frequent mowing to maintain a short sward may be needed on parts of the site to maintain a neat appearance or for recreation. Opportunities for grazing of urban sites is usually limited. Glades, edges of tracks and other open areas can be maintained by cutting in rotation every two to three years. For further details see chapter 7.

Materials and labour

List the planting stock, and any accessories required for weed control or protection. Estimate the labour requirement for planting. This may be done in one season, or as successional planting over a few seasons. For further details see page 71.

Five year plan

Detail maintenance and future work for the next five years. Include a review of progress so that changes can be made if necessary. Detail the responsibilities for maintenance and review of progress.

Woodland design

The balance of tree cover with grassland areas will depend on the priorities for the site. Where timber or coppice production is a primary aim, the proportion of overall tree cover will need to be high. Where woodland grants are being obtained, the amount of tree cover must be within the terms of the grant. For amenity use, the open spaces, avenues, wide paths and other features within a woodland are of great value. For reasons of security against attack, fear of being lost, and simply because the woodland edge is often the most attractive part of a wood, most people like woods with plenty of spaces within them. The woodland edge also attracts a wide range of plants and animals. Open space comprising about one-third of the total area of the woodland gives a reasonable balance.

When designing the planting, retain any existing patterns of hedges, walls, ditches or other boundaries within the site, and give them emphasis by using them as edges to planting plots. Don't plant densely right up to the edges of ditches and streams, but leave a margin of about 5m of bankside vegetation, with occasional trees. The edges of woodland plots, and the landscape features they create, are more important than the shape of the plot in plan view. Within the plots, plant trees at close spacings to ensure good survival, and then thin as required to create the type of woodland you want. Manage the spaces outside the plots as paths, glades, meadows, marshes or ponds.

The following table gives the numbers of trees per hectare at square spacings. It can be used to estimate the number of planting stock required, and the thinning required for final spacings.

SPACING metres	TREES PER HECTARE (1 hectare = 10,000sq metres)
1.0	10,000
1.5	4,444
1.8	3,086
2.0	2,500
3.0	1,111
3.5	816
4.1	600
5.8	300
7.1	200
10	100
14.1	50

WOODLAND TYPE

Types of woodland include coppice, coppice with standards, high forest and parkland or pasture wood. These describe the traditional ways of growing trees, and refer not only to the type of woodland produced, but to the style of growth of an individual tree. These styles of growth, produced by pruning, are just as valid for small groups of trees as for a large woodland. Certain species of trees are particularly suited to each type of growth. Trees can also be grown unpruned, in which case their shape will be determined by their spacing and by factors such as soil and exposure to the wind.

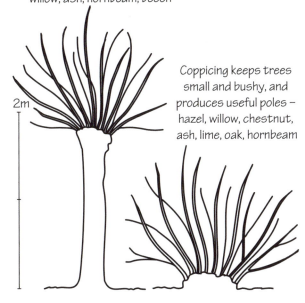

Pollarding restricts the ultimate height and spread of trees, and produces poles or firewood – willow, ash, hornbeam, beech

2m

Coppicing keeps trees small and bushy, and produces useful poles – hazel, willow, chestnut, ash, lime, oak, hornbeam

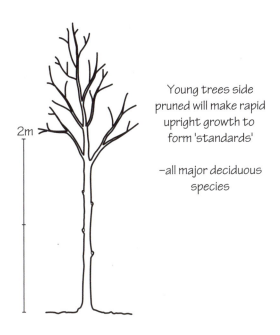

2m

Young trees side pruned will make rapid upright growth to form 'standards'

–all major deciduous species

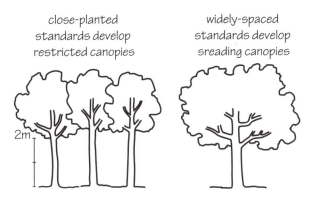

close-planted standards develop restricted canopies

widely-spaced standards develop sreading canopies

2m

Flora locale
Denford Manor, Hungerford, Berkshire RG17 0UN
Tel: 01488 680 457
www.floralocale.org

Forestry Commission GB & Scotland
Silvan House, 231 Corstorphine Road,
Edinburgh EH12 7AT
Tel: 0131 334 0303 (switchboard)
Enquiries: 0845 FORESTS (3673787)
www.forestry.gov.uk

Free Form Arts Trust
274 Richmond Road, London Fields,
London E8 3QW
Tel: 020 7249 3394
www.freeform.org.uk

Friends of the Earth
26-28 Underwood Street, London N1 7JQ
Tel: 020 7490 1555
www.foe.co.uk

Groundwork UK
Lockside, 5 Scotland Street, Birmingham B1 2RR
Tel: 0121 236 8565
www.groundwork.org.uk

Henry Doubleday Research Association
Ryton Organic Gardens, Coventry CV8 3LG
Tel: 024 7630 3517
www.hdra.org.uk

The Greenwood Centre
Station Rd, Coalbrookdale, Telford, Shrops TF8 7DR
Tel: 01952 432769
www.greenwoodcentre.org.uk

Lantra
Lantra House, Stoneleigh Park, Coventry CV8 2LG
Tel: 024 7669 6996
www.lantra.co.uk

Landlife
National Wildflower Centre, Court Hey Park,
Liverpool L16 3NA
Tel: 0151 737 1819
www.landlife.org.uk

Learning through Landscapes Trust
3rd Floor, South Side Offices, The Law Courts,
Winchester, Hampshire SO23 9DL
Tel: 01962 846258
www.ltl.org.uk

LETSLINK UK
LETSlink UK, 12 Southcote Road, London N19 5BJ
Tel: 020 7607 7852
www.letslinkuk.net

Natural England
Natural England, 1 East Parade, Sheffield S1 2ET
Tel: 0114 241 8920
www.naturalengland.org.uk

Neighbourhood Initiatives Foundation
The Poplars, Lightmoor, Telford,
Shropshire TF4 3QN
Tel: 0870 7700339
www.nif.co.uk

Permaculture Association
BCM Permaculture Association, London WC1N 3XX
Tel: 0845 4581805
www.permaculture.org.uk

Plantlife
14 Rollestone Street, Salisbury, Wiltshire SP1 1DX
Tel: 01722 342730
www.plantlife.org.uk

Ponds Conservation Trust
School of Life Sciences, Oxford Brookes University,
Gipsy Lane, Headington, Oxford OX3 0BP
Tel: 01865 483249
www.brookes.ac.uk/pondaction

REACH
89 Albert Embankment, London SE1 7TP
Tel: 020 7582 6543
www.reach-online.org.uk

Royal National Institute for the Blind
105 Judd Street, London WC1H 9NE
Tel: 020 7388 1266
www.rnib.org.uk

Scottish Environment Protection Agency (SEPA)
SEPA Corporate Office, Erskine Court,
Castle Business Park, Stirling FK9 4TR
Tel: 01786 457700

Scottish Natural Heritage
Great Glen House, Leachkin Road,
Inverness IV3 8NW
Tel: 01463 725000
www.snh.org.uk

The Sensory Trust
Watering Lane Nursery, Pentewan,
Cornwall PL26 6BE
Tel: 01726 222900
www.sensorytrust.org.uk

Small Woods Association
Green Wood Centre, Station Road, Coalbrookdale,
Telford TF8 7DR
Tel: 01952 432769
www.smallwoods.org.uk

Sustrans Ltd
2 Cathedral Square, College Green, Bristol BS1 5DD
Tel: 0117 926 8893
www.sustrans.org.uk

Thrive
The Geoffrey Udall Centre, Beech Hill,
Reading RG7 2AT
Tel: 01189 885688
www.thrive.org.uk

Tidy Britain Group
The Pier, Wigan WN3 4EX
Tel: 01942 824620
www.encams.org

The Tree Advice Trust
Arboricultural Advisory and Information Service,
Alice Holt Lodge, Wrecclesham, Farnham,
Surrey GU10 4LH
Tree Helpline: 09065 161147 (*premium rate*)
www.treehelp.info

Tree Council
71 Newcomen Street, London SE1 1YT
Tel: 020 7407 9992
www.treecouncil.org.uk

Waste Watch
56-64 Leonard Street, London EC2A 4LT
Tel: 020 7549 0300
www.wastewatch.org.uk

Waterways Recovery Group
PO Box 114, Rickmansworth, WD3 1ZY
Tel: 01923 711114
www.wrg.org.uk

The Wildlife Trusts
The Kiln, Waterside, Mather Road, Newark,
Nottinghamshire NG24 1WT
Tel: 0870 036 7711
www.wildlifetrusts.org

Woodland Trust
Autumn Park, Dysart Road, Grantham,
Lincolnshire NG31 6LL
Tel: 01476 581111
www.woodland-trust.org.uk

WWF-UK
Panda House, Weyside Park, Godalming,
Surrey GU7 1XR
Tel: 01483 426444
www.wwf.org

Websites

www.adas.co.uk (consultancy and research organisation for the land-based industries)

www.aie.org.uk (Arboricultural Information Exchange)

www.alphasearch.co.uk (index of woodland suppliers, services, training)

www.communityforest.org.uk (Community Forests)

www.communities.gov.uk (Department for Communities and Local Government)

www.ecnc.nl (European Centre for Nature Conservation)

www.ecolots.co.uk (Conservation products, equipment and services, for sale and wanted)

www.jncc.gov.uk (Joint Nature Conservation Committee)

www.naturenet.net (Nature conservation network)

www.nhbs.com (Natural History Book Service)

www.nbn.org.uk (National Biodiversity Network)

www.recycle-it.org (Timber Recycling Information Centre)

www.tree-register.org (Tree Register of the British Isles)

www.treesource.co.uk (tree bookshop and information)

www.treetrader.co.uk (UK native tree nurseries)

www.ukbap.org.uk (Biodiversity Action Plans)

www.woodnet.org.uk (service for wood producers and users)

Bibliography

Abbott, Mike (1989)
Green Woodwork
Guild of Master Craftsman Publications

Ash, H J, Bennett, R, Scott, R (1992)
Flowers in the Grass
English Nature

BT Countryside for All
A Good Practice Guide to Disabled People's Access in the Countryside
Fieldfare Trust

Baines, Chris (2000)
How to Make a Wildlife Garden
Frances Lincoln

Baines, J C and Smart, J M (1991)
A Guide to Habitat Creation
Packard

BSBI and JNCC (1999)
Code of Conduct for the conservation and enjoyment of wild plants
BSBI and JNCC

Broad, Ken (1998)
Caring for Small Woods
Earthscan Publications Ltd

Burgess, J (1995)
Growing in confidence – understanding people's perceptions of urban fringe woodlands
Countryside Commission

Butcher, Mary
Willow Work
Mickle Print

Child, L and Wade, M (2000)
The Japanese Knotweed Manual
Packard, Chichester

Coulthard, Nonie and Scott, Michael (2001)
Flowers of the forest
Plantlife

Dewar, Sue M, and Shawyer, Colin R (1996)
Boxes, Baskets and Platforms – artificial nest sites for owls and other birds of prey
The Hawk and Owl Trust

du Feu, Chris (1993)
Nestboxes
British Trust for Ornithology

Emery, Malcolm (1986)
Promoting Nature in Cities and Towns – a practical guide
Croom Helm

Evans, J (1984)
Silviculture of Broadleaved Woodland
Forestry Commission Bulletin 62

FACT (2001)
Practical Solutions Handbook 2nd edition
English Nature

Ferris-Kaan, R (1995)
The ecology of woodland creation
John Wiley and Sons

Forestry Commission (1994)
The Management of Semi-Natural Woodlands
(A series of 8 Forestry Practice Guides on the management of different types of native woodland)
Forestry Commission

Francis, Joanna L and Morton, Alan (2001)
Enhancement of amenity-woodland field layers in Milton Keynes
In British Wildlife Vol 12 No 4, 2001

Gilbert, Oliver (1992)
Rooted in stone: the natural flora of urban walls
English Nature

Gilbert, Oliver (1992)
The flowering of cities: the natural flora of urban 'commons'
English Nature

Gilbert, Oliver L and Anderson, Penny (1998)
Habitat Creation and Repair
Oxford University Press

Gibson, Tony (1997)
The Power in our Hands
Neighbourhood Initiatives Foundation

Greenhalgh, Liz and Worpole, Ken (1995)
Park Life – Urban Parks and Social Renewal
Comedia in association with Demos

Gulliver, Richard and Gulliver, Mavis
Key to Plants Common in Woodlands
Field Studies Council

Hampshire County Council (1995)
Hazel Coppice – past, present and future
Hampshire County Council

Harrison, Carolyn; Burgess, Jacquelin; Millward,
Allison; and Dawe, Gerald (1995)
Accessible natural greenspace in towns and cities
English Nature Research Report 153

Herbert, R, Samuel G and Patterson, G (1999)
Using Local Stock for Planting Native Trees and Shrubs
Forestry Commission Practice Note

Hessayon, Dr D G
The Garden Expert Series
Pbi publications

Hibberd, B G (edit) (1989)
Urban Forestry Practice
Forestry Commission Handbook 5

Hodge, Simon J (1995)
Creating and Managing Woodlands around Towns
Forestry Commission Handbook 11

Hodge, Simon and Pepper, Harry (1998)
The Prevention of Mammal Damage to Trees in Woodland
Forestry Commission Practice Note

Keech, D et al (2000)
The Common Ground Book of Orchards
Common Ground

Kerr, Gary and Williams, Hugh V (1999)
Woodland Creation – Experience from the National Forest
Forestry Commission Technical Paper 27

Kirby, K J and Drake, M (1993)
Dead Wood Matters
English Nature

Kirby, P (2001)
Habitat Management for Invertebrates
RSPB

Law, Ben (2001)
The Woodland Way
Permanent Publications

Luscombe, Grant and Scott, Richard (1994)
Wildflowers Work
Landlife

Mabey, Richard (1996)
Flora Britannica
Sinclair-Stevenson

Merritt, Antony (1994)
Wetlands, Industry and Wildlife
The Wildfowl and Wetlands Trust

Miles, Archie (1999)
Silva: The Tree in Britain
Ebury Press

Mitchley, J, Burch, F, Buckley, P and Watt, T A (2000)
Habitat restoration monitoring handbook
English Nature Research Report No. 378

Mummery, C, Tabor, R and Homewood, N (1990)
A guide to the techniques of coppice management
Essex Wildlife Trust

National Urban Forestry Unit
Urban Forestry in Practice – Case Studies
NUFU

National Small Woods Association (1998)
Small Woods Information Pack
National Small Woods Association *
(*now the Small Woods Association)

O'Donnell (2000)
Turning Green Wood
Guild of Master Craftsmen

Parker, C M (1995)
Habitat Creation: A Critical Guide
English Nature

Parkes, Charlie and Thornley, John (1994)
Law of the Countryside
Countryside Management Association

Parrott, J and Mackenzie, N (2000)
Restoring and Managing Riparian Woodlands
Scottish Native Woods, Aberfeldy

Peterken, George F (1996)
*Natural Woodland – Ecology and Conservation in
Northern Temperate Regions*
Cambridge University Press

Rackham, Oliver (1986)
The History of the Countryside
J M Dent

Rackham, Oliver (1990)
Trees and Woodland in the British Landscape
J M Dent

Read, Helen J (2000)
Veteran Trees: A guide to good management
English Nature

Rodwell, John and Patterson, Gordon (1994)
Creating New Native Woodlands
Forestry Commission Bulletin 112

Shaw, P (1994)
Orchid Woods and Floating Islands – the ecology of fly ash
British Wildlife 5(3): 149-157

Smart, N and Andrews, J (1985)
Birds and Broadleaves Handbook
RSPB

Sustrans (1994)
Making Ways for the Bicycle
Sustrans

Sustrans
Safe Routes to Schools Information Pack
Sustrans

Tabor, Ray (2000)
The Encyclopedia of Green Woodworking
eco-logic books

Taylor, Michael Bradley
A Guide to Wildlife Law Enforcement in the UK
www.defra.gov.uk/paw

Warnes, Jon (2001)
Living Willow Sculpture
Search Press

Wheater, C Phillip (series editor) (1999)
Urban Habitats
Routledge

Wilcox, David (1994)
The Guide to Effective Participation
Partnership Books, 13 Pelham Square, Brighton

Williams, P et al (1999)
The Pond Book
The Ponds Conservation Trust

JOURNALS

Relevant journals on urban environmental action include:

Arboricultural Journal
(quarterly: from the Arboricultural Association)

British Wildlife (bi-monthly independent magazine)

Clean Slate (quarterly journal of the Centre for Alternative Technology)

Ecolots (www.ecolots.co.uk)

Enact (quarterly: English Nature)

Tree News (twice-yearly: from the Tree Council)

Urbio (three times a year: English Nature magazine on urban biodiversity)

BTCV publications

The BTCV Practical Handbook series was started in the 1970s, with most of the original titles remaining in print throughout, and new titles being added over the years. There is a rolling programme of revision with most Handbooks now in their second edition. BTCV welcomes feedback at any time on any aspect of the Handbooks, whether the comments are general or detailed, practical or academic, complimentary or critical. Please contact:

Handbooks Editor
BTCV, Sedum House, Mallard Way,
Doncaster DN4 8DB
Tel: 01302 388883
e-mail: information@btcv.org.uk

The Handbook series comprises:

Dry Stone Walling (2nd edition, 1999)

Fencing (2nd edition, 2001)

Footpaths (2nd edition, 1996)

Hedging (2nd edition, 1998)

Tree Planting and Aftercare (2nd edition, 2000)

Sand Dunes (2nd edition, 1986)

Toolcare (3rd edition, 2000)

The Urban Handbook (1998)

Waterways and Wetlands (2nd edition, 1997)

Woodlands (3rd edition, 2002)

To order any of the Handbooks, or for details of other BTCV publications and merchandise, please contact BTCV at the address above.

Orders can also be placed through the BTCV website at www.btcv.org/shop

Photography credits

Jane Alexander • Alan Atkinson • Graham Burns • Nicola Davis • Jeff Pick • Mick Weston • Lancashire Wildlife Trust

Sincere thanks to everyone whose photographs have been a valuable record of BTCV's urban work.

Index